BLOOD, BONES and BODY BITS

NICK ARNOLD

Illustrated by
Tony De Saulles

This edition produced for the Book People Ltd in 2006,
Hall Wood Avenue, Haydock, St Helens WA11 9UL

First published in the UK by Scholastic Ltd, 1996

10 digit ISBN 0 439 94333 7
13 digit ISBN 978 0439 94333 8

Printed and bound by Nørhaven Paperback A/S, Denmark

10 9 8 7 6 5 4 3 2 1

Papers used by Scholastic Children's Books are
made from wood grown in sustainable forests.

Contents

HURRY UP!

Nick Arnold has been writing stories and books since he was a youngster, but never dreamt he'd find fame writing about body bits. His research involved inspecting sick, being sucked by thirsty leeches and encountering deadly diseases and he enjoyed every minute of it.

When he's not delving into Horrible Science, he spends his spare time teaching adults in a college. His hobbies include eating pizza, riding his bike and thinking up corny jokes (though not all at the same time).

Tony De Saulles picked up his crayons when he was still in nappies and has been doodling ever since. He takes Horrible Science very seriously and even agreed to investigate what happens in an operating theatre for us. Fortunately, he has made a full recovery.

When he's not out with his sketchpad, Tony likes to write poetry and play squash, though he hasn't written any poetry about squash yet.

INTRODUCTION

Science is sickening! Extra science homework is really rotten – but one of the most horribly sickening science subjects is the science of the body. I mean, doesn't the thought of all that blood and all those guts and bones turn your legs into jelly?

Doctors and teachers use a sickening selection of tongue-twisting names for bits you didn't even know you had. By the way – did you know that medical students have to learn 10,000 new words? And you thought English lessons were tough!

But science doesn't just belong to the experts – it belongs to everybody, because everybody's got a body – and you've got every right to know what's going on in yours. Why it gurgles and creaks and squelches and other tantalising topics.

And that's what this book is about. The things YOU really want to know about YOUR body. The horrible bits. The horribly interesting bits. Here's your chance to find out what billions of germs are doing lurking in your

5

guts. What happens when you cut a brain in half, and why doctors once covered their patients in slimy leeches. So if you find science a closed book – here's a chance to change your mind.

And once you've boned up on bones and got the inside story on your insides – who knows? You might even find the body horribly amazing. Then you could teach your doctor a thing or two. Or even blind your teachers with some really sickening scientific facts. (That doesn't mean doing nasty things to their eyeballs!) One thing is certain. Science will never be the same again!

A disgusting discovery

It was past midnight and the rain was splattering against the window-pane of the lonely attic room. By the dim light of a candle Baron Frankenstein gazed in horror at the creature that he had just put together from bits of chopped-up dead bodies. The monster was unbelievably, hideously ugly. Suddenly a shudder seemed to run through the creature's body and it stirred like a heavy sleeper about to wake. . .

DON'T PANIC! It's only a story. Frankenstein was written by Mary Shelley nearly 200 years ago and no one has succeeded in making an entire human being out of bits of body . . . yet. But just supposing you wanted to have a go, here's a bit of advice. . .

STEP ONE - GET HOLD OF A HUMAN BODY. I STOLE MOST OF MY BODY BITS . . .

If this sounds too gruesome to be true, remember that in the Baron's time there was a serious shortage of bodies to cut up. In many countries this grisly practice was against the law. This was a problem because scientists could only probe the secrets of the human body by the dissection – cutting up – of dead bodies. In desperation, some scientists turned to crime.

The Baron's guide to body-snatching

Body-snatchers were people who went about stealing bodies. The body-snatchers knew that doctors would pay handsomely for a nice fresh corpse to cut up. Here's how to get hold of one yourself (and make some extra pocket money).

Method 1 – execute a robbery. This was the method used by Andreas Versalius, a famous 16th-century scientist, when he was living in the old town of Louvain in Belgium.

1 Wait until dark.

2 Go to a nearby place of execution and remove the corpses of any criminals you find.

3 Cut up the body and hide bits of it under your cloak. That way you can smuggle it all past the guards on the city gates without anyone asking awkward questions.

4 You can hide the bits of body in your bedroom and put them together later.

If you can't find any bodies lying around things get a tiny bit more difficult.

Method 2 – rob a grave. This method was used in both Britain and America in the 19th century.

1 Wait until dark. You will need a wooden spade for silent digging, a lantern, a canvas sheet, some ropes with hooks attached, a crowbar and a sack.

2 Go to a graveyard. Make sure you keep an eye out for angry relatives, vicars, etc. who might just try to stop you digging up the bodies.

3 Dig up the grave. Spread the dug earth on the sheet ready for you to shovel it all back again afterwards. This avoids making a mess that might give you away.

4 Lift the coffin with the hooks, then lever open the coffin using the crowbar. Sssh! Keep it quiet!

5 Put the body in the sack. Fill in the hole and run for it. You should be able to do all this in an hour. Oh, and don't forget the sheet!

Body jigsaws

Let's imagine that by hook or by crook you managed to get hold of some bits of body. Now you can start putting them all together to make your very own Frankenstein's monster! Unlike a normal jigsaw, you have to start with the middle bits, not the edge (the skin!). Make sure you put all the pieces in the right places and don't forget any vital parts or it won't work. If you make a mistake you will have to cut the body open and take a few bits out in order to fit the missing bit in its proper place. Here's a list of body bits to help you know what's what in your body.

Stretchy skin

A huge waterproof, germ-proof outer covering. It's better than any other kind of clothing because it actually repairs itself when it gets damaged. It also has its own heating and cooling systems. Skin wraps round the rest of the body bits to keep them in position.

Fabulous fat

Fit a layer of fat snugly underneath the skin. Slabs of fat also slop and wobble around the tummy and hips area. Fat keeps out the cold. It acts as a convenient place for storing spare sugar from all those sweets your monster eats. Your monster will use up some of the sugar when it goes for its morning jog.

Eyeballs, ears and snotty nose

Very important for seeing, hearing and sniffing (in that order). In fact the really important bits of these body parts are the bits you can't see. These form the high-tech gadgetry that converts the information picked up from the senses into signals for the brain to de-code. So make sure those nerves are all properly wired up.

Other items you will need . . .

Needle and thread for sewing the body together

Saw for cutting a hole to put the brain in

Funnel for pouring blood into the body

Delicate nerves

These are the monster's signalling system. They tell the brain what's going on and transmit orders from the brain to get those lazy muscles moving. Nerves extend into every part of the body – from the top of the head to the tips of the toes. But the main nerves all join up in the spinal cord inside the backbone.

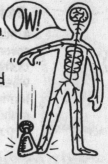

Brilliant brain

This bit acts as the boss of the monster's body. Gently plop it inside the top part of the skull, nicely protected from the outside world. It contains all your monster's memories and personality so don't bash it around too much.

Sturdy skeleton

There are 206 bones – give or take a few extra ones that some people have. Bones are very important to keep the body upright and stop it collapsing like a deflated balloon. Make sure you get the bones in the right order. This is very tricky, especially when you get to the 26 bones that make up a single foot.

Mighty muscles

BULGE

AWFUL
UNDERPANTS

Everyone's got muscles even if they're not big bulgy ones. There are hundreds of muscles and they need to be put in their rightful places or they won't work properly. In each hand there are twenty muscles – and your monster will use 200 muscles every time it takes a step.

Tough teeth

These are the hardest parts of the body – guaranteed to tackle those rubbery school dinners. Make sure you put the teeth in their correct positions and teach your monster how to brush them regularly.

Disgusting stomach

The stomach is a squelchy muscular bag filled with bits of half-digested food and stomach juices. Lovely! Your monster will need guts to digest its dinners – that means take the chemicals its body needs into its blood.

Lovely liver

It's a brownish/purplish/reddish blob about 15cm thick. Lovely. This is your monster's built-in chemical factory and it performs over 500 different jobs. It's called the liver because no-one can 'liver' long without it, ha ha. Pop the liver in its place over the guts under the dome of the diaphragm (that's your breathing muscle).

WIBBLE WOBBLE

Clever kidneys

These filter the blood and take out the waste products from your monster's body. It's got two kidneys and the one on the left-hand side of the body is always higher up than the right one.

Beautiful blood

It's the body's transport system, and it carries oxygen gas breathed in through the lungs and little bits of food to nourish the body. And that's just for starters. There are also white cells that fight germs and platelets that help the body heal itself. Yes – blood's got the lot. Your monster will need about 5 to 5.5 litres (8.8–9.7 pints) of the gloopy red stuff.

Hardworking heart

This lump of muscle is vital for pumping the blood around the body. Make sure you put the heart in its correct place – nearer the left side of the chest. Also make sure you get it the correct way round – the left-hand side of the heart pumps the blood round the body, but the right side only pumps it round the lungs.

Foamy lungs

These are like a big spongy pair of bellows in the chest that can hold up to six litres of air. Your monster needs to breathe in order to get the oxygen from the air to keep its body cells alive.

Weird bits 'n' pieces

Some bits of the body are well known. We've all heard about the brain and we've all heard from the stomach when it starts rumbling. But what about the not-so-well-known bits? Which of these bits are just too weird to be true? (You get double the score if you can work out where any of them fit in!)

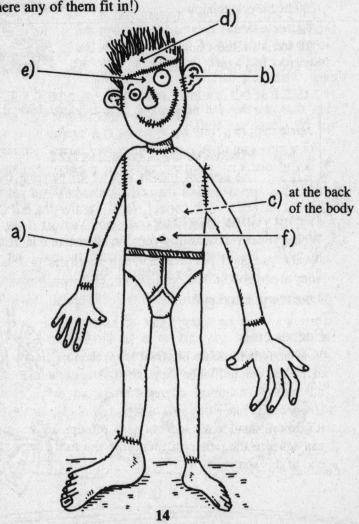

d)

e)

b)

c) at the back of the body

a)

f)

1 The oval window
2 The funny bone
3 The innominate canal of Arnold
4 The wish bone
5 The boomerang bone
6 Fabricus's ship
7 The bicycle tendon
8 Lane's kinks
9 Morris's kidney box
10 The fossa of Blumenbach

Is everything working?

Whilst you are assembling your Frankenstein's monster, it's always a good idea to occasionally check that the bits of body are in good shape. You can do this by peering down a microscope and making sure the cells are still alive. . .

Secret cells

Your body is made up of about 50 million million living cells. You can tell when they are alive because there are all sorts of chemical changes going on inside them. Every cell is like a tiny ball of jelly full of chemicals and it's far too small to see without a microscope. In fact, you can squeeze thousands of them into the full stop at the end of this sentence.

Inside the cell is a secret world. There are tiny objects called mitochondria (mito-con-dre-a) that produce energy, and there are pathways and little storage areas. And each cell has a nucleus that stores the information to make new cells. Sometimes the cell reproduces by pulling itself into two pieces.

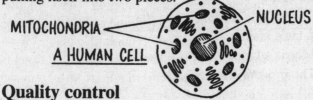

MITOCHONDRIA

NUCLEUS

A HUMAN CELL

Quality control

Once your Frankenstein's monster is assembled you'll need a collection of amazing but slightly gruesome tools to check whether everything is in working order inside.

X-rays

You'll need X-rays to check whether your monster's bones are in good shape. These are high-energy rays that you can't actually see. They can pass through the body's skin, muscles and fat but not solid bone. This is why an X-ray picture can check out whether the bones are in good shape.

YOU APPEAR TO HAVE SOMEONE ELSE'S BONES SIR!

CAT – computerised axial tomography scanner. This amazing machine scans a slice of your monster's brain using X-rays and shows the result on a computer screen.
Angiogram (An-gy-o-gram) An X-ray picture of your monster's blood vessels after they have been injected with chemicals.

MRI – magnetic resonance imaging – this high-tech bit of kit uses a combination of super-powerful magnets and radio waves to create a 3-d computer image of your monster's insides. And you can even use this marvellous machine to make a gruesome movie of your monster's heart pumping blood.

Then there are a whole collection of tubes to stick into various parts of its anatomy so you can take a look at it. These include…

Gastroscope (gas-tro-scope) A long, bendy tube with a light on the end. Ideal for poking down its throat to see into its stomach and guts.

Ophthalmoscope (op-thal-mo-scope) A bright light and viewer to see what the inside of its eyeball looks like.

Arthroscope (ar-throw-scope) A tube a bit like a telescope for peering inside your creature's joints.

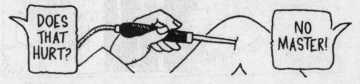

Otoscope (ot-o-scope) A light a bit like a torch for shining in your monster's ear-holes.

All these bits of equipment are useful because without them it's horribly hard to see what's going on inside the body. There's usually a layer of sweaty skin in the way. Let's take a longer look at it. . .

‑SWEATY SKIN‑

Poke around in the darker corners of your house and you may find a lovely collection of fingernails, hair and bits of skin. Bits of skin? Well – you know those pretty bits of dust that dance in the sunlight on a summer's morning? Most of them are bits of flaked-off skin – just some of the ten billion bits of skin you lose every day!

Skin fact file

Name of body part: Skin

Where found: All over the outside of the body

Useful things it does: It helps to keep you at the right temperature and keep out germs.

Grisly details: It suffers from a disgusting array of skin diseases such as boils, carbuncles, etc.

Amazing features: If you removed an adult's skin it would cover about 2 square metres (2.4 square yards). A child's skin covers about 1.5 square metres. Skin is the heaviest part of your body and weighs a whopping 2.5-4.5kg (5-10lbs), depending on your size.

Disgusting skin diseases

Doctors like nothing better than reading at mealtimes. And their favourite reading matter? Colourful medical magazines with pictures of skin diseases. Gulp! Here's your chance to check whether you could be a doctor. Try matching the picture to the disease:

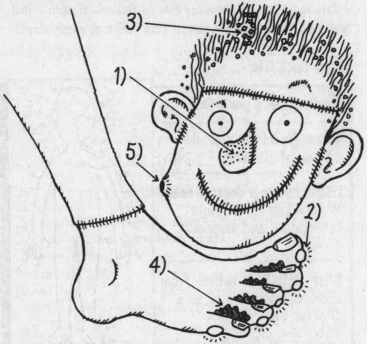

a) A fungus that grows between the toes and makes the skin peel.

b) A gland-opening that's been blocked with sweat or grease – it swells until it bursts, spraying pus everywhere.

c) Painful, itchy blotches on your toes caused by the blood supply cutting off in cold weather.

d) A build up of dead skin cells stuck together with grease.

e) Greasy dead skin cells that turn black when they come in contact with the air.

Nasty nose jobs

If your skin disease gets really revolting you could have plastic surgery to replace some of it.

Bet you never knew!
Modern plastic surgeons make changes to the surface of the body – adding or taking away skin in order to change what someone looks like. If you've got enough money, you can change almost any part of your body. But plastic surgery actually began in India about 2,000 years ago! Criminals were punished by having their noses cut off but one day someone found out that you could stitch some skin from the forehead or cheek over the wound so it didn't look so bad. In Sicily, Italy, they took the idea one stage further. A sinister surgeon named Branca cut off a slave's nose and sewed it onto one of his patients who had lost his own nose in a battle! Modern plastic surgeons use skin from the patient's own body to repair damage to the skin caused, for example, by burns. These operations are called "skin grafts".

But if skin can be amazingly horrible on the outside – on the inside it's also horribly AMAZING.

Getting under your skin

Imagine walking around all day with a heavy bag of shopping from the supermarket. Well, you do – it's the weight of your skin. But your skin is well worth hanging onto – just look what's in it! Your skin's outer layer is less than 1 mm (0.04 inches) thick but it's packed with useful bits and pieces such as blood vessels and nerves. An area of your skin the size of a ten pence coin has around 65 hairs, 100 oil-producing glands, 650 glands that produce sweat and 1,500 nerve sensors (see page 23). Sounds confusing? Try imagining your skin as an incredible high-tech, high-fashion space-suit. Would you dare to wear it?

The Birthday Suit

Have YOU ever wished to slip into something more comfortable? Something that's cool in hot weather and warm in cold weather. Try the new birthday suit. But guess what - you've got it on already! Yes, it's that suit you got for your birthday – that's the day you were born!

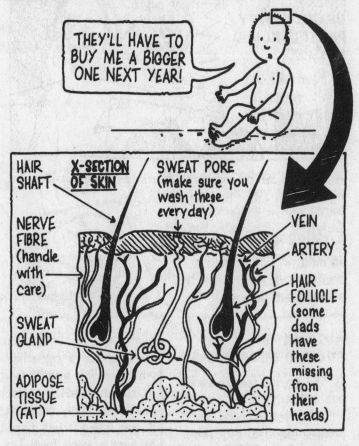

Marvel at these incredible features. Amaze your friends with THE BIRTHDAY SUIT's unique technical wizardry!

The amazing
BIRTHDAY SUIT

UNIQUE SAFETY PHOTOCHROMIC COLOURS

1. Your BIRTHDAY SUIT comes in a variety of colours all provided by its unique melanin pigments.

2. Ordinary clothes fade in the sunshine but your BIRTHDAY SUIT comes with a guaranteed darkening action under sunlight to protect the wearer from harmful rays. It actually creates extra melanin for this all-important purpose.

GET ONE FREE WITH EVERY NEWBORN BABY!

NO FADING

FRONT

CHOICE OF COLOURS

AUTOMATIC COOLING MECHANISM

3. This unique feature springs into action if the suit gets too hot. The water-cooling pipes produce sweat to cool the outside of the BIRTHDAY SUIT.

4. Every BIRTHDAY SUIT is guaranteed to contain about three million of these tiny water-cooling pipes (known as sweat glands) and each one is so tightly coiled that if you pulled it out it would be over a metre long! The total length of your pipe system is 3660km (2269 miles)!

5. The automatic cooling systems can easily lose 1.7 litres (quarter of a gallon) of sweat every hour in hot weather, so make sure it's well supplied with water.

6. The sweat under the arms and between the legs contains chemicals that germs like to eat. Yum! The germs make the stale sweat all yucky and smelly. (Please see Care and maintenance instruction 9 – for everybody's sake.)

7. Some people use deodorants to tackle the little problem above. These work by blocking the holes in the cooling systems. Fortunately they don't stop most of the sweat from escaping otherwise the BIRTHDAY SUIT would overheat.

SELF-
REPAIRING
MECHANISM

AUTOMATIC
COOLING
SYSTEM

BACK

LOW
MAINTENANCE

HARMFUL RAY
PROTECTION

CARE & MAINTENANCE INSTRUCTIONS

8. Your BIRTHDAY SUIT needs very little maintenance because of its unique self-repair mechanism. If it gets torn or damaged it will simply re-grow!

9. All you need to do is to gently wash the outer layer in soap and water to remove any dirt and flaky bits. Don't worry if bits drop off – the BIRTHDAY SUIT will always grow some more underneath!

Dare you find out for yourself . . . how your skin works?

For this experiment you will have to take a hot bath. It's OK – all the great scientists had to make sacrifices.

1 Note what happens as your skin heats up. What colour does it go?

a) Red

b) Blue

c) White

2 Using a watch, time how long it takes for your skin to wrinkle up. As a result of your careful scientific observation, what do you think is causing this strange effect?

a) The heat

b) Old age

c) The water

Answers 1 a) The colour is due to the blood vessels that run under the skin widening to allow more blood in. This helps release heat through the skin and cools your over-heating body! **2 c)** Your skin is covered by a layer of oily grease called sebum that keeps the water out. But after a while some of the water seeps through and makes the under layer waterlogged. This crumples up the top layer causing wrinkles. It's a bad idea to let too much water get under the skin. The cells absorb all the water they can until they explode! Lucky your hair and nails are not affected.

HORRIBLE HAIR AND NASTY NAILS

What's the point of hair and nails? Hairs always seem to end up blocking the bathroom plug hole and nails get nasty black grime stuck underneath them. But then they're also interesting in a disgusting kind of way.

Hair and nails fact file

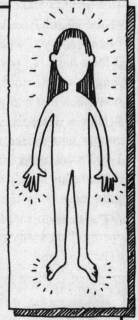

Name of body part: Hair and nails

Where found: Your body is covered by five million little hairs but your longest hairs are on your head (surprisingly!). Nails are found on your fingers and toes, but you knew that.

Useful things they do: Hair keeps you warm. Your nails stop your fingers and toes squashing up every time you touch something.

Grisly details: Hair and nails are said to continue to grow for a while on dead bodies.

Amazing features: Hair and nails are both made out of a hard substance called keratin. It's the same stuff that makes feathers and dinosaur claws.

Hair-raising hair

Here's your chance to hoodwink your hairdresser with a few hair-raising facts.

1 Most people have about 100,000 hairs on their heads. Fair-haired people can have 150,000 and red-haired people have to make do with about 90,000. (I wonder who counted them all!)

2 Hair grows at about 1 cm a month or 0.33 mm a day. Hot weather makes your hair grow faster. So if you lived at the North Pole you wouldn't need your hair cut so often – and you wouldn't want it cut so often.

3 Most hairs fall out before they reach 90 cm (35 inches) long. It's quite normal to lose up to 60 hairs a day. Any more than that and you might start going bald!

4 Hair is horribly strong. One hair is stronger than a copper wire of the same thickness. A rope made from 1,000 hairs could lift a well-built man.

5 Your hair stands on end when you're scared because little muscles in the skin pull on the roots of the hairs. The aim is to make you look big and fearsome to an enemy. That's why cats fluff their fur when they're going to have a fight!

GOSH – HE LOOKS BIG AND FEARSOME!

Nail-biting notes

Now mystify your manicurist with these nails' tales.

1 Underneath your nails is an area called the nail bed. (not the bed of nails that Indian fakirs sometimes sleep on.) Your nails grow from an area called the matrix.

2 If you trap a nail in the door it will stop growing and drop off. With a bit of luck a lovely brand new nail will grow underneath. That's OK then!

3 Sometimes toenails start burrowing into the surrounding flesh. This horribly hurtful condition is caused by not cutting the nail straight across. But cutting nails is better than biting them!

4 Nail biting doesn't exactly kill you – but it looks revolting and makes your nails sore, and it helps lots of germs leap into your mouth. It also tends to put people off their soup in posh restaurants. Especially when you chew your toenails as well!

5 If you didn't cut your nails for a year they would be 2.5 cm (one inch) long.

But that's nothing compared to some people!

Record-breakers

Longest finger nails Sridhar Chillal of Pune in India stopped cutting his finger nails in

1952. By 1995 the nails on his left hand had reached 574 cm (226 inches) long.

Longest hair Mata Jagdamba of India has hair 4.23 m long. This is amazing because, as we've already said, normally a hair will stop growing and drop out by the time it reaches 90 cm (35 inches).

Longest beard Hans N. Langseth of the USA grew a 533 cm (209 inches) long beard. Sadly, Hans is no longer with us – he died in 1927. But you'll be relieved to know that the famous beard is now a museum exhibit.

PROPERTY OF MR H.N.LANGSETH

Longest moustache Kalyan Ramji Sain of Sundargarth, in India has been growing his moustache since 1976. In 1993 it was 339 cm (133 inches) wide.

Runner-up: A Briton, John Roy, started growing his moustache in 1939. By 1976 his moustache was 189 cm (74 inches) wide. But then he sat on one side of it in the bath and 42 cm (16 inches) of hair split off the end.

MY LIFE'S WORK'S JUST GONE DOWN THE PLUG HOLE!

Bet You Never Knew!
Even with hair all over it, your skin can sense things that touch it. Oh, so you DID know that! Well, bet you never knew that the human fingertips are so sensitive that they can feel an object move even if it only stirs a thousandth of a millimetre. Sounds like a really touchy subject! And touch is just ONE of your five sense-sational senses.

YOU'RE OUT – YOU MOVED AT LEAST ONE THOUSANDTH OF A MILLIMETRE!

COME ON DAD – IT'S ONLY MUSICAL STATUES!

SENSATIONAL ✌ SENSES

Congratulations! You're a sensitive person – how could you be anything else with your super-sensitive touch, sight, taste, smell and hearing? And whether your view of the world is happy or sad, your senses help make sense of what's going on around you. But they're also horribly incredible in their own right – in fact they're SENSE-ATIONAL!

Sensitive senses quiz

Which senses are too sensationally sensitive to be true?

1 Your senses are so sensitive that they only take a quarter of a second to let you know when something is happening. TRUE/FALSE

2 Your eyes can tell the difference between eight million colours. TRUE/FALSE

3 Your eyes are 1,000 times more sensitive to light than the most light-sensitive film. TRUE/FALSE

4 Some people can see ultra-violet rays produced by the sun. TRUE/FALSE

5 Your tongue can taste a single drop of lemon juice even if it's mixed up with 129,000 drops of water. TRUE/FALSE

6 Your nose can detect a cheesy old pair of socks 200 metres (219 yards) away. TRUE/FALSE

7 Your ears can tell the difference between two sounds even if they are only ten-millionths of a second apart. TRUE/FALSE

8 Your ears can identify 1,500 levels of sound from high-pitched squeaks to deep booms. TRUE/FALSE

9 Some people can hear air whooshing around in the upper atmosphere. TRUE/FALSE

10 Your body can tell what time it is even if you're in a room without windows. TRUE/FALSE

Answers: 1 FALSE – your senses work much faster than that! **2** TRUE. **3** TRUE. **4** FALSE and don't try it. Looking at the sun can harm your eyes! **5** TRUE. **6** FALSE – but I suppose it depends on how strong the socks pong! **7** TRUE – if the sounds come through separate ears. **8** TRUE. **9** Supposedly TRUE but unproven – half a mark for this answer! **10** TRUE.

Your touchy senses

You've heard about the sensitive sensors under your skin? Well, did you know that they too come in no less than FIVE sensational varieties? Each one keeps you in touch in a different way.

To show you how, we need a brave volunteer. Can you

spot which sensor is doing the sensing in the five tests below?

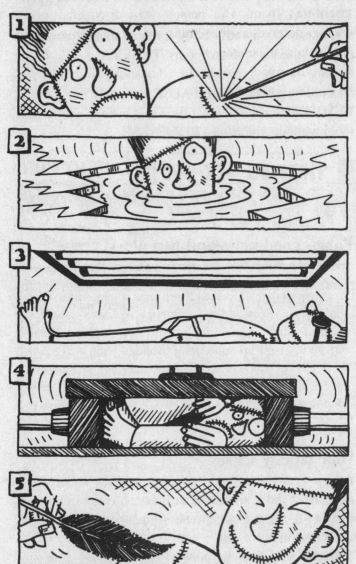

These are the sensors that you must match with the pictures. Some are named in honour of the scientists who discovered them. The person who discovered nerve endings deserves a special mention – it must have been a very painful experience.

a) Heat receptors – for heat

b) Cold receptors – cold

c) Nerve endings – pain

d) Meissner's receptors – touch

e) Pacinean receptors – pressure

Answers: 1 c) 2 b) 3 a) 4 e) 5 d)

Pain – good news and bad news!

You might think that the nerve endings that bring you painful feelings are only there for the nasty things in life. And you'd generally be right. But surely there's some good in everything?

The good news – 1
You have 500,000 sensors to keep you in touch with the outside world. Hooray!

The bad news – 1
And millions of nerve endings to make you painfully aware of any horrible aches and twinges. Boo! Hiss!

The good news – 2
But luckily your brain has its own built-in pain-killers called endorphins. This is why a soldier can lose a leg in battle and hop along without feeling any pain! Hurray!

The bad news – 2

Afterwards it hurts A LOT – and not only that. People who lose arms and legs often feel their missing limbs itching even when they're not there! <u>Shame!</u>

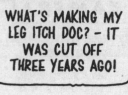

The painful truth

Pain is there to warn us that we're getting hurt. "Stop!" say your nerve endings. "And try to be more careful next time!" It's a sensible message. So you see, a bit of pain is good for you! Sounds a bit like the sort of thing your teacher might say, doesn't it? But is that good news?

A sensational sight

Your most sensational sense is sight. After all, without it we'd all be in the dark! But did you know that your eyeballs are like tiny little video cameras full of watery jelly? Is this the sort of camera that you'd like to discover in your Christmas stocking?

The eyeball camera

Seeing really is believing with the incredible EYEBALL CAMERA. Now you can keep up with the speediest sporting action even at night! Just point your camera in the right direction. Wherever you go, your EYEBALL

CAMERA goes too! In fact, it's so useful it's worth you using the two that you've already got – you know, those gloopy blobs that sit snugly in your eyeball sockets!

THE EYEBALL CAMERA

High-tech gadgets

1 Just behind the iris is a self-adjusting lens for focusing on objects near and far.

2 Your Eyeball Camera has no less than 130 million light-sensitive cells squeezed into an area the size of a postage stamp.

3 Nerves carry the picture to your computer screen (or brain)!

Unique protection features

1 A self-closing eyelid dust cap protects your Eyeball Camera when not in use.

2 Your Eyeball Camera lens is protected with a clear disk. No more nasty little flies spoiling your lovely clear pictures.

3 The lens of your Eyeball Camera is further protected by an iris ring. (lovely choice of colours!) Automatic iris hole-shrink mechanism stops you getting dazzled by bright lights!

FREE MOVING PARTS

1 Your Eyeball Camera is the only camera in the world that's full of water! It's got wobble-free jelly in the front section for a really clear view of life!

2 An incredible extra. Six slim muscle handles hold your Eyeball Camera securely and allow it to swing about without falling on the floor!

Dare you find out for yourself . . . how your eyeballs work?

Naturally you'll want to try out your sensational eyeball camera as soon as possible. So here are a few tests to try.

Test 1: Seeing in the dark

You will need a darkened room, a torch and a tomato. Shine the torch at the tomato and then away from it. What happens to the colour of the tomato as you shift the light away from it? Any idea why?

a) The tomato appears red both in the light and out of it. This is because the eye sees colour in the dark.

b) The tomato appears red in the light and grey out of it. This is because the eye can't see colours in the dark.

c) The tomato appears red in the light and blue out of it. This is because the dark confuses those little light-sensitive eyeball cells.

Test 2: Test your pupils*

You will need a darkened room and a mirror with a light over it. Wait in the room until your eyes are used to the dark. Cover your left eye with one hand and switch on the light over the mirror. Your uncovered pupil suddenly goes smaller. What's happened to your other pupil?

a) It's still large.

b) It's also gone small.

c) It's got even bigger.

* Or you might prefer to test your teacher's pupils – you'll be getting your own back!

Hold the book close to your face and close your left eye. Focus your right eye on the left eyeball. Now slowly move the book away from your face. Why does the right eyeball vanish?

a) The eye can't focus at a certain distance.

b) There's a gap in the light-sensitive cells.

c) The light-sensitive cells get tired and stop noticing things.

Answers: 1 b) There are seven million light-sensitive cone cells inside each eyeball that can see colour (either red, green or blue). But these only work in good light conditions. There are 124 million rod cells that work in dim lighting but they can only see in black and white. **2 b)** The pupils have to work together – it's a bit like being at school! **3 b)** There is a blind spot and when you look at things with it they seem to disappear. This spot is where the optic nerve connects with the inside of the eyeball.

Caring for your eyeballs – eight things you should know

1 You don't need to care for your eyeballs at all! Your body does it all for you.

2 Eyeballs come complete with their own windscreen-washing service – it's called "crying".

3 Fortunately you don't have to be sad to cry. You can produce tears whilst being sick, coughing, or by getting something in your eye or, preferably by laughing!

TRAGIC – SHE ONLY WON THE _SECOND_ PRIZE OF £10,000!

4 Tears are also spread over your eyeball when you blink. Every blink takes 0.3-0.4 seconds – that's half an hour each day, or more than one whole year of your life. What a blinking waste of time!

5 Any tears you don't use dry up in the drainage tube that leads from the corners of your eyes to the inside of your nose. These dried-up tears form the sleepy dust you rub from your eyes every morning!

6 Each of your eyes is protected by about 200 eyelashes. Each eyelash lasts three to five months before it falls out and another grows in its place.

7 Tiny mites live in the base of your eyelashes. They have eight legs each and look like alligators! But don't worry – they won't do you any harm. In fact they are doing you quite a favour by gobbling up harmful germs!

8 If, despite all this care and attention, your eyes don't see very well – you may need glasses.

Savage spectacles

One of the first people to wear "glasses" was the rotten old Roman Emperor Nero. He used a curved piece of emerald to help him enjoy the savage spectacle of lions tearing people apart at the Roman games. That sounds like really bad taste. . .

FAR OUT!

Terrible tastes and sickening smells

Here's the problem with taste and smell. They're sensational senses all right. They bring you some sensational sensations like your favourite foods and the smell of roses. But they also bring you foul bitter tastes and sickening stinks!

Terrible tastes

To find out more about taste you've got to peer into your

wet drooling mouth. Better take a look now before you chicken out!

Look closely at your tongue. Say Aghhhhhh! Can you see those little bumps and lines? The little lines are crammed with 8,000 or so taste buds linked to the brain by nerves. Different buds handle sweet, sour, salty and bitter tastes.

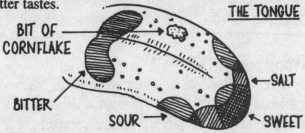

THE TONGUE

BIT OF CORNFLAKE

BITTER

SOUR

SALT

SWEET

The really tasteless question is – why are you supposed to taste bitter things at all? I mean – how many bitter-tasting foods do you actually like enough to eat? Well, you're not actually meant to eat most of them – spitting them out would be a lot better for you. This is because most poisons taste bitter, so the bitter-sensitive taste buds are there to tell you that you're just about to eat some vile POISON.

YOU WANT THE **BITTER** TRUTH?
...HE'S BEEN POISONED!

Sickening stinks

Your smelling equipment is a 2.5 cm-square patch in the top part of the area behind your nostrils. This patch has over 500 million tiny thread-like sticking-out bits called cilia (silly-ah).

Cilia have a really sickening job – they hang around in groups of eight from rod-like trunks buried in snot. (Yuck!) Smells take the form of tiny bits (called molecules) that float about in the air. When a smelly molecule lands on one of the cilia it triggers a chemical change that's passed on as a signal to the nerves.

Sensationally sensitive

Your sense of smell is sensationally sensitive. It's actually 10,000 times more sensitive than taste! That's OK when there's something nice to be sniffed but there are some really revolting odours around. And did you know your nose can sniff one molecule of the stinky juice squirted by a skunk even when it's mixed with 30,000,000,000 molecules of fresh air?! Yeuch!

Bet you never knew!
People lump taste and smell together because. . .
1 They work together to help you appreciate the delicious flavour of your favourite foods.
2 In fact when you're eating your favourite fries and thinking, These are sensationally scrummy-tasting chips, *you're actually smelling them!*
3 If you couldn't smell them they'd probably taste like cardboard!
4 That's what happens when you have a snorting stinker of a cold. Your nose is blocked up by snot and because you can't smell, your food doesn't taste like it should! Sounds horrible!

Silly sound detectors

Ears are eerie things. After all, just think how odd some people's ears look. And guess what? They're even odder on the inside! Just listen to this. . .

How the ears work

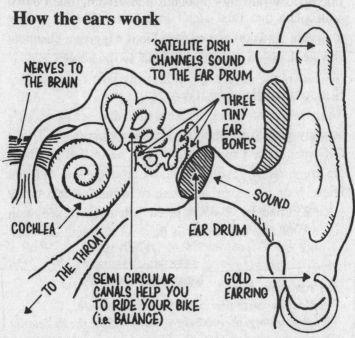

'SATELLITE DISH' CHANNELS SOUND TO THE EAR DRUM

NERVES TO THE BRAIN

THREE TINY EAR BONES

SOUND

COCHLEA

EAR DRUM

TO THE THROAT

SEMI CIRCULAR CANALS HELP YOU TO RIDE YOUR BIKE (i.e. BALANCE)

GOLD EARRING

The ears work like a couple of satellite dishes linked up to a drum, linked up to a triangle and stick linked up to a microphone with a carpenter's level attached! Simple, isn't it?

1 Like satellite dishes, your ears pick up signals in the air and bounce them into the central hole. With your ears, the signals in question are sounds.

2 The eardrum's a bit like a real drum. It trembles when sounds hit it.

3 The trembling eardrum makes the tiny ear bones jangle just like a triangle hit by a stick.

4 The cochlea picks up the sounds and makes them into nerve signals that go to the brain. It's a bit like a microphone picking up sounds and sending them down a wire.

5 Like a carpenter's level, the semi-circular canals are full of liquid that sloshes around as your head moves. Sensors in the canals stop you losing your balance. This is good news for tight-rope walkers!

An urgent horrible health warning

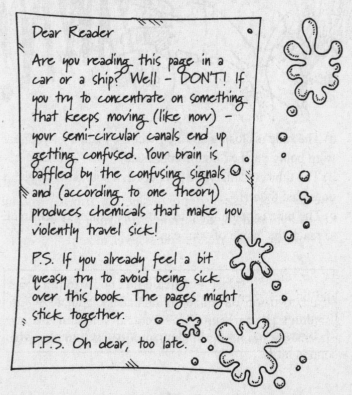

Dear Reader

Are you reading this page in a car or a ship? Well – DON'T! If you try to concentrate on something that keeps moving (like now) – your semi-circular canals end up getting confused. Your brain is baffled by the confusing signals and (according to one theory) produces chemicals that make you violently travel sick!

P.S. If you already feel a bit queasy try to avoid being sick over this book. The pages might stick together.

P.P.S. Oh dear, too late.

Dare you find out for yourself . . . why your ears go POP?

Try listening to yourself yawning. You may hear a few tiny tingling pops at the start of the yawn – keep trying if you don't hear them at first! So what causes them? Clue: it's something to do with your eustachian (you-station) tube – a useful little tunnel linking your mouth with the inner parts of each ear.

a) The tube is closing up to protect the insides of your ear from being yawned out of your head.

b) The tube contains little poppers that sound off when air goes past them.

c) The tube is opening up to allow the extra yawned-in air to reach the inside of your ear.

Answer: c) Normally the tube is closed but it opens if the air pressure increases at either end. Examples might include when you suddenly go down or up a steep hill or when you breathe in deeply.

Taking leave of your senses

Each one of your senses is unique and sensational in its own way. But they all have one thing in common. They all need someone or something to talk to and give them a quick answer. So they send all their information to the same place – your very baffling BRAIN.

THAT MAKES SENSE!

THE BAFFLING BRAIN

Your brain is baffling. Baffling, bemusing, bewildering and brain-bogglingly bamboozling. For instance, how can this 1.5 kg (3 lbs) of pinkish-grey blob be more powerful than the most powerful computer in the entire known universe? Everything it does is baffling – including its mystifying memory and strange sleeping habits.

CLICK BUZZ WHIRR

WATKINS – WHAT IS 7693271 ÷ 15134?

508·34353 SIR!

What does the brain do all day?

Now there's a baffling question. Unlike other parts of the body it doesn't seem to do anything exciting like squirt blood, leap about or fight germs. It just sits there wobbling nervously. It looks like a watery blancmange and it even squelches if you poke a finger in it and waggle it about.

But the brain is always busy. Even when it doesn't seem to be doing much your brain is crackling with the electrical force of millions of nerves – just tell that to your teacher next time she accuses you of daydreaming! Your brain fires off signals, feelings, orders and thoughts at incredible speed. And in order to perform at such baffling speed your brain needs some strong nerves . . . lots of them.

Nerves fact file

Name of body part: Nerves

Where found: Form a network throughout the body but mainly in the spine and connecting to the brain

Useful things they do: Take info from your senses to your brain. Bring orders from your brain to the rest of your body.

Grisly details: You can wire a battery to nerves in a chopped-off finger and make it twitch. There's one for the school science lab!

Amazing features: Nerves can carry signals at 100 metres (109 yards) a second – that's one of their slower speeds!

Speedy signals

Nerve messages are electrical signals zipping down the nerve cells and leaping from cell to cell. Phew – sounds tiring! The nerve cells don't actually touch one another. Signals are passed on by chemicals that leap the gap between cells and spark an electrical pulse on the other side.

Reckless reflexes

Most of the signals from your nerves go to your brain to
tell it what's going on in the different parts of your body.
But some messages move so fast that they make you do
things before you realise it and control it. Sounds like a
good excuse for doing something really reckless – like
breaking things!

But if reflexes are moves you make without thinking,
which of these aren't reflexes?

1 Snatching a hand
away from the heat

2 Blinking

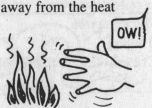

3 Riding a bicycle

4 Sneezing

5 Getting washed in the morning

6 Hair standing on end when scared

7 Rolling the eyes

8 Eating breakfast

Dare you find out for yourself . . . how to test your reflexes?

Have you been hit below the kneecap by a doctor wielding a small rubber hammer? If so – it was probably to test the nerves that cause a reflex that works when you're walking. Here's how to do it yourself.

1 Rest one leg loosely over the other.

2 Lightly tap the upper leg just below the kneecap. What happens next?

a) The leg jerks forwards.

b) The leg jerks backwards.

c) A small purple patch appears on the lower leg.

I SAID **SMALL RUBBER** HAMMER!!

Reflexes are alright as far as they go. But to do anything interesting you need to ask your baffling brain.

Baffling brain fact file

Name of body part: Brain

Where found: Inside the top part of your skull.

Useful things it does: Bosses the rest of your body about. In charge of your memories, thoughts, dreams, etc.

Grisly details: Your brain cells started dying off as soon as you were born. And many of them aren't getting replaced.*

Amazing features: The brain is more than 80 per cent water!

*Fortunately you've got 15,000 million cells up there ~ more than enough for a long life-time! That's:

• Three times more than a gorilla.

• Seven million times more than a stick insect.

• And about 900 million times more than a small worm that sometimes lives in the human gut.

Teacher's brain tour

If the brain is incredibly baffling on the outside – the inside is even more baffling. It's like a big office building (even your teacher's is quite big) with lots of rooms filled with people doing things you don't understand. Well, here's a guided tour of your teacher's office block – I mean – brain.

Note: Don't touch anything on the tour as it might give your teacher a brainstorm! And don't remove any of your teacher's brain cells either – he hasn't got enough to spare!

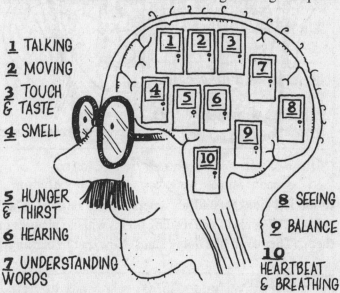

1 TALKING
2 MOVING
3 TOUCH & TASTE
4 SMELL
5 HUNGER & THIRST
6 HEARING
7 UNDERSTANDING WORDS
8 SEEING
9 BALANCE
10 HEARTBEAT & BREATHING

1 The cerebrum (ser-re-brum)

Includes your teacher's library where his or her murky memories are stored. Also the boss's office where decisions are made, and offices for the speech, hearing, moving, touch, sight, understanding and feelings (probably a very small office in this case) departments.

2 Two separate halves

Many of these offices are split into two halves linked by communication cables. In the right half the staff are artistic and emotional. They enjoy painting and arranging flowers.

In the left side the staff are scientific and rational. They enjoy playing chess and reading books with no pictures in them. (They even like doing sums. Now that IS baffling!)

3 Thalamus

This is the switchboard that relays information from all your senses to the brain.

4 Limbic (lim-bick) system

This is where your teacher's feelings are checked to make sure he can feel anger, fear, sadness – and even happiness. (Yes – teachers do occasionally experience this emotion.) The staff make sure your teacher doesn't get so happy he walks around with a silly great grin all day.

5 Cerebellum (serry-bell-um)
Staff here control your teacher's more skilful movements. OK – there aren't too many of these.

6 Under-brain
This is another switchboard for transferring news about reflexes happening elsewhere in your teacher's body.

7 Hypothalamus (hi-po-thal-a-muss)
In this broom cupboard are the controls for your teacher's sweating, growing, sleeping and waking, thirst and hunger control systems. There's also the control panel for the sympathetic and parasympathetic systems. It's a big job for a little office!

8 The pineal (pi-knee-al) body

No one knows what goes on here. Perhaps it's your teacher's time-control system. It may tell your teacher to wake up in the morning and to stay awake through your science lesson! No – DON'T reset these controls!

Be a brain scientist

Can you use your knowledge of how the brain works to predict the results of these baffling brain experiments?

Experiment 1 In the 19th century, French scientist Paul Broca weighed 292 male brains and 140 female brains. He concluded that on average female brains weighed 200 g (7 ounces) less than male brains. How would you explain this result?

a) Men are cleverer than women.

b) Boys are more big-headed than girls.

c) Men have bigger heads than women.

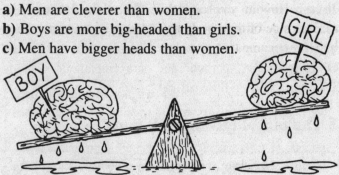

Experiment 2 In 1864, two French doctors were discussing what happens to the brain after the head is cut off. As luck would have it one of the doctors was due to have his head chopped off shortly. So the condemned doctor bravely agreed to try winking his right eye three times in response to a shout from his friend. But what was the result of this grisly experiment?

a) The head stuck its tongue out.

b) Nothing – because the brain was dead.

c) The head winked once.

Experiment 3 Some surgeons cut the nerves connecting the two halves of the cerebrum in order to combat brain disease. How do you think this affected the patients?

a) Each side of their body acted like a separate person.

b) They became twice as clever.

c) They died.

Dare you find out for yourself . . . how your friend's brain works?

Reassure your friend that this experiment does not

involve any pain. And they won't need to have their head cut off either. Absolutely not. But you do need to remember some rather baffling information.

• The left side of your vision is linked to the right side of the brain and vice-versa.

• The left side of the cerebrum is the half that imagines where to find something.

• The right side deals with maths questions.

1 Write down five or more baffling maths questions.

2 And write another list of five or more baffling requests to give directions from one place to another, e.g. from home to school.

3 Don't tell your friend the aim of the experiment. Stand facing them about three paces away.

4 Ask your friend a maths question followed by a whereabouts question until you have completed both lists.

5 Watch their eye movements. What happens?

a) Their eyes roll upward before they answer the whereabouts questions and go cross-eyed with the maths questions.

b) Their eyes go right for the maths questions and left for the whereabouts questions.

c) Their eyes go left for the maths questions and right for the whereabouts questions.

How to baffle your teacher

Here's how to baffle your maths teacher with your amazing brain power.

1 Ask your maths teacher the answer to the sum 4 divided by 47. Try to sound rather casual as if you've just thought up the question.

2 Make sure your teacher doesn't cheat by using a calculator.

3 After a lengthy pause for thought your teacher should be able to come up with something like 0.08 or even 0.085.

4 Smile sweetly and say,

"I don't think that's quite right. I think it's 0.08 510638297872340425531914893617021276595 74468."

5 Pause to savour the expression of shock on your teacher's face.

6 Hopefully your teacher won't realise that this incredible feat of mental arithmetic has already been performed by Professor A.C. Aitken of Edinburgh University.

7 Of course, if you don't happen to be a mathematical genius you'll have to learn the answer off by heart. (Tip: it's easier if you learn the numbers in groups of three or four and then string them together.)

Baffling learning

One of the most baffling things your brain does is

learning. It's incredible how they expect you to learn so much. Children at school have to learn on average TEN new words every day! But that's nothing! For example, Bhanddanta Vicittabi Vumsa of Burma learnt 16,000 pages of religious text off by heart.

PAGE 14,763 IS FASCINATING . . .

Russian journalist Solomon Veniaminoff never forgot anything he learnt in his entire life!

AS YOU WERE SAYING 42 YEARS AGO . . .

Learning is all about remembering things. But the really baffling thing about learning is that scientists don't quite understand how memory works! Or maybe they can but they can't remember. But it's thought to involve electrical and then chemical changes within the brain cells. Or something like that. It's all very vague . . . and very baffling.

The baffled brain

The baffling brain is easily baffled. Just take a look at the picture below – is it a vase or are they two heads? See what I mean? Your brain just can't make up its mind.

Bet you never knew!
Brain bafflement can easily result from a bash on the head. For the brain this can be a deeply baffling experience involving loss of memory or even loss of consciousness. The damage is caused by the violent movement sloshing the poor old brain about. When one girl banged her head she started writing backwards ... and was only cured when she banged her head again cheering her favourite football team on the telly!

No laughing matter

Chemicals such as pain-killers can also baffle the brain. Some just deaden pain without knocking you out, but the more powerful pain-killers actually cause the brain to lose consciousness. So who invented these powerful drugs? Well, it's a painful story.

Once upon a time surgeons performed operations without any pain-killers. They would cut off your leg or whip out vital portions of your anatomy and all you got was a gag to stop you screaming too loudly! But that was before Mr Horace Wells got in on the act.

Connecticut, United States, 1844

Horace Wells was deeply in on the act. And he wished he wasn't. The act in question was a display showing the effects of laughing-gas and Horace was in the audience. But Horace Wells wasn't really watching the show at all because he was busy being in agony. The plump, smartly dressed dentist was suffering from the most embarrassing ailment for anyone in his profession . . . toothache. It was so annoying – that he, the great Horace Wells – the inventor of a wonderful new solder for fixing false teeth should have to endure this awful indignity.

He made another effort to concentrate on the entertainment. Laughing-gas, or nitrous oxide, as scientists called it had been discovered about 70 years before. And it didn't just make you laugh. A few whiffs had even the most outwardly boring person singing, dancing, fighting, talking nonsense or even passing out. The hugely popular laughing-gas shows employed bouncers to protect the audience from the crazy antics of volunteers who breathed the gas.

Suddenly, one of the volunteers went berserk. There was a struggle and the man got injured – but he didn't seem to feel any pain!

Lucky you, thought Horace Wells nursing his aching jaw. Then a little light bulb flashed inside his head and for the first time that evening he smiled. (Just a bit – you can't smile too easily with toothache.) If laughing-gas could deaden pain and knock you out . . . then perhaps . . . perhaps just maybe. . .

After the show Horace Wells approached the organiser with a somewhat baffling request.

"Could you lend me some laughing-gas?"

Wells hoped to knock himself out whilst another dentist removed the aching tooth. In those days pulling out a tooth was a painful and rather bloody job involving a huge pair of tongs and a great deal of tugging. But Horace Wells breathed in the gas and didn't feel a thing!

"It's a new era for tooth-pulling!" he exclaimed in triumph as the effects of the laughing-gas wore off. Or that's what he meant to say but since his mouth was still sore the words probably came out as,

ITCH AR HUGH HIERA FUR HOO-FARLIN!

Yes, he, Horace Wells was about to sell the pain-killing secret of laughing-gas and become rich and famous. Seriously rich.

But the pain-killing project came to a rather painful conclusion. The first public use of laughing-gas by a dentist ended in disaster when the patient woke too soon. He had received too little gas. During a later operation another patient died after receiving too much gas. A few years later Horace Wells himself came to a painful end. He went mad as a result of breathing too much pain-killing gas and in 1848 he took his own life. But he didn't die in vain. Today the idea of using a pain-killing gas (not laughing-gas!) in medicine is well-established.

Fortunately you don't need to rely on gas to send you to sleep.

Your brain's baffling bedtime

Every night at about the same time your brain does something remarkable – and quite baffling. It winds down its operations, pulls down the shutters and more or less switches itself off. Yes, that's right, it goes to sleep. Altogether your brain will spend at least 20 years in this odd condition. Why? Well, the really baffling bit is that no one really knows!

HURRY UP – I WANT TO SWITCH OFF!

All you need to know about sleep – in three easy lessons

In order to make sleep less baffling here is a course of sleep lessons. It's taught at night school, of course, and unlike ordinary school, the teachers don't mind if you nod off!

Lesson 1 – falling asleep

1 Make sure you are neither too hot nor too cold. It helps if you go to bed at the same time each night.

2 Lie very still with your eyes closed. Try counting backwards from 1,000 or imagining yourself on a lovely relaxing holiday.

3 You'll notice that you can't pin-point the moment when you fall asleep. Some people feel they are falling and twitch violently at this point so they have to start all over again!

Lesson 2 – what happens when you're asleep?

1 Here are a few things you ought to know before you fall asleep. Whilst you are sleeping. . .

- Your body temperature starts falling.
- Your weight drops by 28-42 g (1-1.5 ounces) each hour.
- You can change position up to 40 times a night.
- You can wake up for less than three minutes at a time

and you probably won't remember it in the morning.

2 Don't worry about listening out for danger whilst you're asleep – your brain does this job automatically.

3 Here are some things you shouldn't do whilst asleep.

• Try not to sleep walk – about one in 20 children do this.

• Try not to snore too loudly. This disgusting din is made by someone sleeping on their back with their mouth open. As they breathe in, the wobbly bits at the back of their mouth start rattling noisily.

4 You can stop snorers by putting something hard and prickly (such as an old hair-brush or hedgehog) into the bed. The snorer rolls onto his back and the prickles wake him up!

5 After about 90 minutes of sleep your eyeballs start twitching but the nerves to most of your muscles shut down so you can't move. You are about to enter the most baffling part of your sleep – the DREAM ZONE.

Lesson 3 – exploring the dream zone

1 Welcome to a strange world where time and space have no meaning and where nothing is impossible.

2 Dreams are caused by signals fired towards your brain by nerves underneath it. When you are awake this area screens out boring sounds – that's why you don't notice

traffic or your teacher droning on and on and on.
Zzzzzzzzz.

3 Most dreams take 6-10 minutes but the record for the longest dream is 150 minutes! During your 20 years asleep you can look forward to watching 300,000 dreams!

4 Every night you make several trips to the dream zone.

5 Some good and bad dream news. THE GOOD NEWS: Happy dreams are three times more common than sad dreams. THE BAD NEWS: As it gets towards morning you are more likely to encounter nightmares. If you're reading this in bed you'd better save the next chapter till morning – you don't want to dream about ghastly groaning skeletons now, do you?

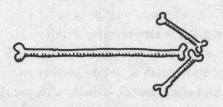

BONES ⟨ AND ⟩ GROANS

Bone up on bones

Spooky stories are full of groaning skeletons. But skeletons don't groan for the fun of it. No. They're groaning because that's what bones do to you. They ache and they break and if you happen to have muscles attached to your bones they ache even more! Funnily enough, bones make some scientists groan too. Well – imagine having to remember all 206 bones in the human body! Here are a few of the more memorable groans – er, I mean bones.

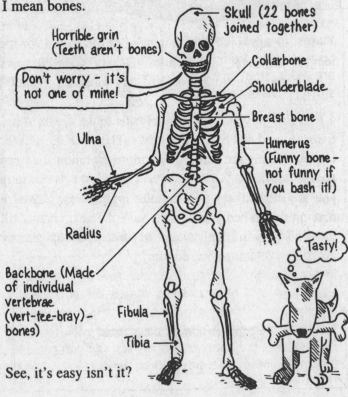

Skull (22 bones joined together)

Horrible grin (Teeth aren't bones)

Don't worry – it's not one of mine!

Collarbone

Shoulderblade

Breast bone

Ulna

Humerus (Funny bone – not funny if you bash it!)

Radius

Backbone (Made of individual vertebrae (vert-tee-bray) – bones)

Fibula

Tibia

Tasty!

See, it's easy isn't it?

Bones fact file

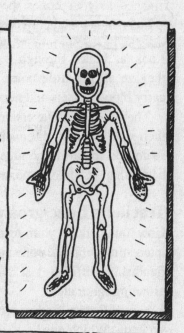

Name of body part: Bones

Where found: Your bones form the skeleton that makes up about 25 per cent of your weight. Bones are made from a tough stringy substance called collagen (collar-gen), and strengthened with a mixture of hard materials.

Useful things they do: They hold your body upright and give your muscles something to pull against.

Grisly details: If you took all the minerals out of your thigh bone you could tie what's left in a knot.

Amazing features: A broken bone repairs itself. As long as the broken ends are "set" or put back together – new bone grows over the break.

Bones – the inside story!

Some bones are solid with an area of spongy bone on the inside, others are long and hollow and their empty centres are filled with juicy jelly-like red marrow. Dogs love marrow because it's full of meaty goodness. So should you. Your marvellous marrow makes you 173 BILLION brand new blood cells every day.

Look at bones through a microscope and you'll see they've all got little holes in them. These tiny tunnels carry blood vessels and nerves.

They're called Haversian canals (Have-er-shun) after their oddly-named discoverer – Clopton Havers. It may seem odd to call these tiny tubes "canals" but it sounds better than ' Clopton's bone-holes" at least.

Teacher's bone-groan test

How much does your teacher really know about this interesting subject? Bone up on the answers to this ultra-fiendishly difficult test and show up your teacher's groaning ignorance!

1 You will only find one of these bones in the human skeleton. Which one?

a) The tail bone

b) The elbow bone

c) The nose bone

2 If you wanted to hold up a heavy weight what would be the strongest thing to use?

a) A stone pillar

b) A concrete pillar

c) A leg bone

3 A giraffe has seven bones in its neck. How many neck bones has a human got?

a) 3

b) 7

c) 12

4 How many bones does a baby have?

a) 206, just like a grown-up person.

b) 86

c) More than 350

5 Some Tibetan priests use the skull as a drinking cup. How much liquid do these creepy cups hold?

a) 500 ml

b) 1.5 litres

c) None – it trickles out through the eye-sockets.

6 What bone forms the sticking-out bit of your ankle?

a) The bottom of the tibia

b) The ankle bone

c) The top of the heel bone

7 What is a wormian bone?

a) A wiggley little bone in the little toe.

b) An extra bone sometimes found in a baby's skull.

c) A bone infested by worms.

Answers: 1 a) Yes – that's right! We've all got tails! The coccyx (cox-sicks) is a mass of three to five joined-up bones at the end of the backbone. Fortunately it's not long enough to poke outside the body! **2 c) 3 b)** The giraffe bones are much longer! **4 c)** Lots of these extra bones join up as the baby grows up. **5 b) 6 a) 7 b)**

What your teacher's score means:

0-3 Make no bones about it – your teacher is a bone-head!

4-5 Your teacher can teach you a few facts but only knows the bare bones of the subject.

6-7 Your teacher is probably an osteologist* (ost-tee-ol-o-gist). He or she may even have a real human skeleton at home for study purposes.

* An expert on bones.

Bet You Never Knew!
An osteologist studies bones looking for clues that can identify the person to whom the skeleton belonged. Do you think you could do this? Here's your chance to use your skills to solve a truly horrible true mystery.

The wandering bones

It was 7 December 1976, Long Beach, California. The TV cameraman was in for a nasty shock. He was in a haunted house side-show filming a TV series. As he moved a gruesome dummy away from the rest of the film crew – its arm fell off! The arm was real. And there was bone underneath!

The police were called but it soon became clear that this was no ordinary dummy – it had once been alive! The police discovered three fiendish facts. The body had been pickled in the deadly poison arsenic. It had been shot by an old-fashioned type of bullet dating from before 1914. In the body's mouth was a coin dated 1924.

The police then traced a series of former owners of the

body. The former owners (who had all thought the body was a dummy) were colourful showmen who scraped a living exhibiting the gruesome specimen at funfairs. The oldest showman thought he could remember buying the body in Oklahoma. Then local history buffs dredged up a possible identity for the butchered body – Elmer McCurdy, cowboy and outlaw.

Elmer McCurdy's luck had run out at dawn on 7 October 1911. When the sheriff's men came for him he was drunk with stolen whiskey and exhausted after a night spent hiding in a hayloft. A young lad was sent up to the hiding place.

"The boys want you to surrender, Mister!" he cried.

"I'll see them in hell first!" roared the outlaw.

McCurdy died with his boots on after slugging out a desperate gun battle until his six-gun was empty. After the outlaw's death an undertaker had preserved the body and charged people to see it propped against his parlour wall!

Many people tried to buy the body but all offers were refused. Then the undertaker gave the body away to a nice man who said he was Elmer's long-lost brother.

Three months later the body appeared in a street-show in Texas.

But could the police bone experts prove that the body actually belonged to McCurdy? Here is a description of the outlaw dating from 1911. Which of the following features might you be able to check by examining the bones inside the body?

WANTED

FOR ROBBING TRAINS
ELMER McCURDY
(ALIAS FRANK CURTIS)
HAVE YOU SEEN THIS MAN?
1. Male
2. Age about 29-35
3. Height 170cm (67 inches)
4. Bearded
5. Thin nose
6. Deep set eyes
7. Slim build
8. Right-handed

Answers: 1 Yes, females have wider pelvic bones. **2** Yes, as he grew older some of his bones joined together. **3** Yes, by the length of the thigh bones. **4 5 6** No. **7** Yes, by looking at the build of the skeleton. **8** Yes, marks on the right arm bones showed traces of more developed muscles than on the left side.

After studying the bones the scientists were certain they

had the right man. The final proof came when they found that an old photo of the outlaw's head perfectly matched the shape of the skull. And so, at long last, Elmer McCurdy's body was given a decent burial – nearly 66 years after he was killed!

Join up the joints

Could you be a bone expert? If so you'd need to know how to fit a skeleton together. The bones in a skeleton fit together to form joints and the trick is to assemble the joints correctly. But it's not easy – there are over 200 joints to join up!

Here are the main types of joints.

1 Hinge joint. Joints such as the knee work like door hinges, allowing the bones to move backwards and forwards. But they don't move so easily from side to side.

2 Gliding joint. The ankle bones can easily slide up and down and from side to side.

3 Ball and socket joint. As the name implies this is a ball and socket that allows arm and thigh bones to move in most directions.

4 Swivel joint. This joint allows the bone on top to move up and down and from side to side.

5 Saddle joint. The bone on top is like a jockey on a saddle. So it sways about and leans in all directions – without falling off!

Lucky ligaments

Imagine if your arm fell off every time you threw a ball! This doesn't happen because tough cords called ligaments hold your bones together over the joint. Contortionists stretch their ligaments as they bend their bodies into horrible positions. You'd groan if you tried this! But did you know that your ligaments and joints allow you to scratch every part of your body? This is lucky if you don't have anyone to scratch your back. Try scratching your own back some time – but NOT during Science class.

Juicy joints

Your joints are surprisingly quiet. They don't groan – they don't even squeak. You can tiptoe softly because every major joint is cushioned in a bag of squelchy liquid. The liquid allows the joint to move smoothly and the ends of the bones are also padded with a softer material called cartilage (karta-lidge). The same stuff forms the bridge of your nose – but if you saw it in a chicken bone you'd call it "gristle".

Moaning muscles

No matter how supple your joints are – you can't make a move without using your muscles. THE GOOD NEWS is that you've got over 600 of them. THE BAD NEWS is that they can make you moan in aching agony!

Groaning muscles fact file

Name of body part: Muscles

Where found: Under the skin and surrounding various body bits.

Useful things they do: They're ALWAYS hard at work squeezing the food through your guts, pumping blood and so on.

Grisly details: Muscles can squeeze so strongly that they break your bones! But they have sensors to stop them squeezing that much!

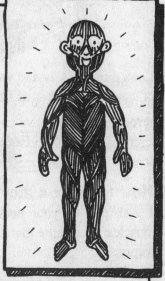

Amazing features: Muscles are anchored to bones by tough tendons. A tendon won't go Twaang! unless you hang a 58-tonne weight from it!

Getting to grips with muscles

To get to grips with your muscles you need to take a closer look. A much closer look. . .

If you cut a muscle in half you can see that it's made of thick bundles of stringy fibres.

Look more closely and you'll see that a fibre is made up of smaller fibres called fibrils.

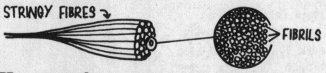

How to make a move

1 Ask one of your nerves to send a signal to your muscles. Make sure that the tiny fibrils are shortening in response.

2 Check that your blood contains enough sugars to provide the energy to power the muscle.

3 The muscle contains chemicals that produce energy by breaking up the molecules of sugar.

But before you move a muscle there are few more things you should know. . .

Groaning muscle facts

1 Muscles have complicated, instantly forgettable Latin names. See if you can remember these.

a) Gluteus maximus – bottom. Makes a nice cushion for sitting on.

b) Digital flexor – wags your finger at people.

c) Levator labii superior – helps you to snarl. Just say the word and you'll be snarling!

2 Muscles can pull but they can't push. That's why muscles work in pairs. One muscle pulls one way and the other muscle pulls in the opposite direction!

3 You can watch the tendons pulling your muscles. Just spread your fingers and waggle them up and down.

4 When you stick your tongue out there's no muscle doing the pushing from behind. A muscle pulls across the tongue and this pushes the tongue forward.

5 As people get older tough stretchy fibres build up inside the muscles. That's why giants and monsters don't like eating stringy old grandparents. They prefer a succulent tender CHILD! Help!

Groans at the gym

Well, be honest, how far can you run? Or does exercise – any kind of effort – make you groan? Are you one of those people who prefer lazing around on the sofa with a big bag of popcorn? Well, if so, you'll be pleased to hear that exercise can be BAD for you! Every sport should carry a Government Health Warning.

Horrible Health Warning 1 Getting off the sofa is dangerous! Your heart suddenly has to pump blood up to your brain and not along a level. Sometimes your brain doesn't get enough blood and you feel dizzy. That's why aircraft pilots sometimes faint on a sudden turn.

I WISH YOU WOULDN'T DO THAT CAPTAIN!

Horrible Health Warning 2 Even when you're up-and-running it's horribly hard work for your body. Your poor feet and ankles have to put up with a pressure of SIX times your body weight. The arches of your feet flop down as they hit the ground. Your fat wobbles, your brain squelches and even your eyeballs bounce slightly in their sockets!

FLOP   SQUELCH   WOBBLE   BOUNCE

Horrible Health Warning 3 Violent exercise is especially bad for you . . . it can cause some especially groan-worthy pains.

a) If your heart beats more than 175 beats a minute it could get injured... Slow down gently!

b) Stiffness. May be caused by loss of water due to sweating and build-up of a chemical called lactic acid in tired muscles . . . Slow down gently after exercise and enjoy a long drink.

c) Cramp is when your muscles squeeze painfully and you can't stop them . . . Keep the muscle warm and rest it. A nice hot-water -bottle will do!

d) Stitch. Caused by cold and running on a full stomach . . . Keep warm. Don't guzzle so much!

I PREFERRED BEING A COUCH POTATO!

But if there's one thing worse than taking exercise it's NOT taking exercise. Look what you miss out on.

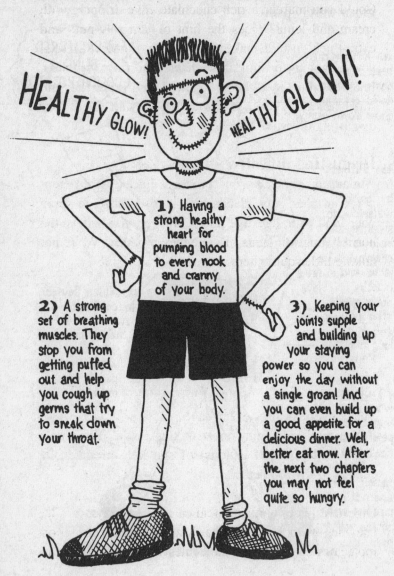

HEALTHY GLOW! HEALTHY GLOW!

1) Having a strong healthy heart for pumping blood to every nook and cranny of your body.

2) A strong set of breathing muscles. They stop you from getting puffed out and help you cough up germs that try to sneak down your throat.

3) Keeping your joints supple and building up your staying power so you can enjoy the day without a single groan! And you can even build up a good appetite for a delicious dinner. Well, better eat now. After the next two chapters you may not feel quite so hungry.

⸰DISGUSTING DIGESTION⸰

Could you murder a rich chocolate cake dripping with cream and icing? Does the hint of jam roly-poly and extra-thick custard make your tummy thunder? If so – you're going to find this chapter horribly tasteless. Imagine your food being chewed and squashed and squelched as it's taken into your body. It's all due to your disgusting digestive juices.

Disgusting digestive glands

A gland is a body bit that produces juices. At different points in your guts, glands lurk – just waiting to spray your food with digestive juices. But can you believe the horribly huge amounts of juice they produce? We're not talking little squirts here. . .

Gland	Daily Squirt
Saliva glands	2 litres *
Stomach	1-2 litres
Pancreas	1-1.5 litres
Liver	1 litre
Lining of guts	2.5 litres

That's over 8.5 litres every day!

* You end up gulping most of this down! Yes, that's 50,000 litres (5,500 gallons) of spit in a lifetime! Or enough to fill 100 baths!

Digestive juices contain chemicals called enzymes. The enzymes work horribly hard to break up the food molecules into smaller molecules that your body can absorb more easily. The hotter the body gets the faster these changes happen, until at 60°C they suddenly stop. Mind you, if you ever got that hot you'd be cooked anyway!

Dare you find out for yourself . . . how enzymes work?

Rennet is a sloppy substance that contains rennin – an enzyme also found in the human stomach. Make sure it's OK for you to use the ingredients below and get someone to help you use the hob.

852 millilitres (1.5 pints) of fresh full cream milk
Sugar
Rennet – available from supermarkets
Saucepan
Bowl
Tablespoon

1 Heat the milk in the saucepan and stir well until it's warm but not hot. DON'T BOIL IT!
2 Pour the milk into the bowl and stir in one tablespoon of sugar.

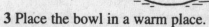

3 Place the bowl in a warm place.
4 Very gently stir in one tablespoon of rennet. Don't touch the bowl for ten minutes.

5 Ten minutes later . . . what's happened to the milk?

HORRIBLE HINT: If your experiment has worked, the rennin will have digested the milk.

a) It's turned into a disgusting smelly yellow mixture with soggy white lumps in it.

b) It's turned into a solid wobbly mass.

c) Nothing

Answer: b) And it's delicious served cold with cream! (If you can bear to eat it.) If c), then the milk was too hot for the enzyme to work.

A horribly healthy diet

Are you a fussy eater? Your body is! To stay healthy your body has to digest a balanced diet. That means all the types of food shown below and NOT just the ones you like!

1 Fibre helps your guts grip your food and keep it moving on its long trek to the toilet.

2 Proteins help your body build and repair its cells. Ten per cent of your body is made of this stuff.

3 Carbohydrates (car-bo-hi-drates) are found in starchy foods. Once they're digested they become sugars that your cells turn into energy.

4 Sickly sweet sugars are less vital, I'm sorry to say. These sugars provide your body with easy energy. Your lazy body feeds the sugar straight to the cells.

5 Fat is a useful store of energy and it helps build body cells - often in a wobbly layer around your tummy.

A sickening sandwich

Could you combine foods that contain fibre, proteins, carbohydrates, sugars and fat in a ONE sandwich snack?

HAM AND JAM SANDWICH

Here are some possibilities.

1 A ham and jam sandwich with a fizzy drink.

2 An egg and baked beans wholemeal-bread sandwich (yuck!) and a mug of hot chocolate.

3 A chip sandwich with white bread followed by treacle pudding washed down with loads of lemonade (burp!).

4 A healthy wholemeal lettuce sandwich followed by a sugar-free nut bar and a glass of mineral water.

A horribly unhealthy diet

As if digestion isn't horrible enough just look at the horribly unhealthy things that some people eat.

1 Some people eat earth. This is horribly unhealthy because it's teeming with germs and tastes disgusting.

2 In 1927 a woman complained of stomach pains. She was rushed to hospital in Ontario, Canada. There, doctors found that she'd swallowed 2,533 objects including 947 bent pins.

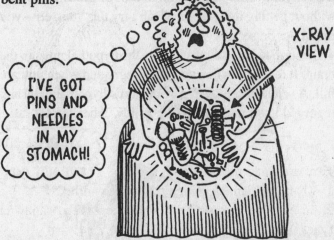

I'VE GOT PINS AND NEEDLES IN MY STOMACH!

X-RAY VIEW

3 But the prize for the most disgusting diet must go to Michel Lotito of France. In his own country he is known as Monsieur Mangetout (Mr Eat-it-all). Since 1966 Mr Eat-it-all has chomped his way through. . .

He generally eats 900 g (31 ounces) of metal a day. All without getting indigestion. (Don't try this yourself – you might not be so lucky!)

4 The urge to eat is controlled by the hypothalamus in the brain. It tells you when you are hungry and when you are full. A scientist removed part of a rat's hypothalamus and it gorged itself until it was a horribly unhealthy fat rat.

THE SCIENTIST

5 At this moment millions of people are trying to lose weight by dieting. But people don't actually need to lose weight unless they are horribly unhealthy. Like William J. Cobb, for example.

In 1962 William J. Cobb weighed 364 kg (57 stone). He was so round that he could only roll like a barrel. Not surprising – considering he was carrying 91 kg (14 stone) of fat! So William decided to go on a diet and within a year or two he was down to 106 kg (16 stone, 7 lbs). He had lost the weight of three large men!

LARGE BAR OF CHOCCY

HEALTHY STICK OF CELERY

BEFORE   AFTER

6 Most people can only lose about half their normal body weight. This takes about three weeks if the person doesn't eat. Then they die – and that's a really unhealthy thing to happen!

Horribly healthy diet complications

To stay horribly healthy you need more than a balanced diet. You've got to eat things that you can't see or taste – like minerals for example. Luckily you don't have to go around looking for minerals to eat. Ordinary food contains minerals in tiny amounts – and that's all your body needs! For example, slurp a milk shake and you're doing your bones a favour. Milk contains the bone-building minerals calcium and phosphate. Then there are other chemicals called vitamins and they're really VITAL.

Vital vitamins

Vitamins are vital because if you don't get enough of them in your diet you become horribly unhealthy. Feel more like gobbling up those greens now?

Vitamin	Found in:	Not enough causes:
A	Milk, butter, eggs, fish oil, liver.	Lots of illnesses and you can't even see in the dark.
B1 and 9 other B vits.	Yeast and wholemeal bread. Also found in milk, nuts and fresh vegetables.	Victim loses energy and can't get out of bed – sounds worse than a Monday morning.
C	Oranges and lemons. Fresh fruit and vegetables.	Loss of teeth, bleeding gums, dark spots on body. Bad breath. Yuck!
D	Oily fish, dairy products.	Bent bones and bandy legs. Bad news for footballers.
E	Wholewheat bread, brown rice and butter.	Scientists aren't quite sure about this one.
K	Green veg, liver	Blood doesn't clot properly – very messy!

It took scientists a great deal of trial and error to discover the disgusting effects of lack of vitamins. But solving these medical mysteries gave them something to crow about.

The sick chickens mystery
Christiaan Eyckman was at his wit's end.

In 1884 he had gone to Indonesia to study a mystery disease. The locals called it, "I can't."

He injected animals with germs thought to cause the disease. The animals stayed healthy!

Then his pet chickens went down with the disease.

He moved them to another place and they got better!
But why?

Maybe they just needed some fresh air.

Or maybe it was due to a change in diet? In their first
home the birds were eating boiled rice.

Now they were eating brown rice.

It turned out that the brown outer layer of the rice
grains was rich in Vitamin B. This prevented, "I can't"
or as we call it, beri-beri.

Mind you, it took Eyckman many years of experiments to prove that eating the wrong rice had made the chickens sick. As for the chickens themselves – things could have been worse. Imagine if something had gone wrong with their digestive bits and pieces. They'd have been sick as parrots then! Yes, we're talking about the gruesome guts!

THE GRUESOME GUTS

Guts are gruesome. Gobsmackingly, grossly, stomach-churningly sickening. In fact – if you thought too much about where your food went you wouldn't feel like eating it! But if there's one thing even more gruesome than guts, it's the scientists who find guts fascinating. Oh yes, and then there's the smelly stuff that pours out the other end. Yuck!

Gruesome guts fact file

Name of body part: Guts

Where found: Mostly under the chest area in the lower part of the body. (See below.)

Useful things they do: Absorb your food once it has been digested.

Grisly details: The guts form a continuous tube up to 8m (8·7 yards) long. That's longer than a huge slithery snake!

Amazing features: Your guts are held in place by the mesentery (mes-en-terry). This stops the guts slopping about and tying themselves in knots!

Dare you find out for yourself ... what's inside your mouth?

Open wide! Here's where it all begins. The gobbling, munching mouth – grinding up the goodies before they hit the guts. Imagine what it's like to be a bit of food!

Tooth truths

The first thing you'll have to worry about are those gigantic spit-dripping jaws. They're made from enamel and they're so tough you need a diamond to drill into them. Inside each tooth there are nerves and blood vessels just like any body part. Not all teeth are the same – there are different-shaped teeth for different jobs. Here are a few that we picked up from a dentist's floor.

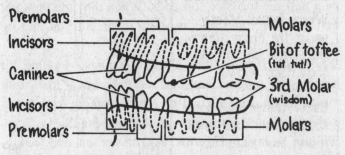

So how many teeth have you got? It depends on how old you are. You started off with 20 teeth that appeared when you were very young. As you get older these fall out and new teeth push through your gums. Here are some tooth totals – which is closest to your own number of teeth?

1 Incisors   a) 2   b) 8   c) 4

2 Canines   a) 2   b) 4   c) 8

3 Pre-molars   a) 4   b) 8   c) 12

4 Molars   a) 4   b) 8   c) 12

Can you spot any of these in your mouth?

Uvula (You've-yer-la) This horrible little wobbly bit spends its time hanging around in your mouth. The name means "little grape" – can you see why? No one knows exactly why it's there but it does help you swallow.

UVULA

Mouth lining If you look at this through a microscope you will see loads of soft cells. When they die they fall into your spit and you swallow them. So you end up eating yourself!

Frenulum (Fren-u-lum) This is the nasty-looking bit under your tongue. You can see the vessels that bring blood to your tongue and give it the energy to talk and taste your food (sometimes at the same time!).

Plaque A layer of germs that cluster on our teeth – they're responsible for tooth decay and bad breath! (If you find any, brush it off!)

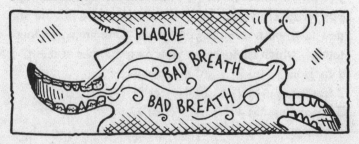

Gruesome gobbling

Once you've checked your mouth – get ready to swallow. Oddly enough most of us manage to do this without thinking. This is probably because swallowing is a reflex action. But it's also a horribly complex operation – see if you can do it by following these instructions. (NOTE: try not to dribble all over your nice clean book.)

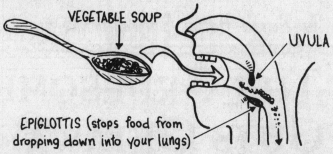

VEGETABLE SOUP

UVULA

EPIGLOTTIS (stops food from dropping down into your lungs)

1 Using your tongue press some food you chewed earlier on to the roof of your mouth.

2 Force the food towards the back of your throat.

3 Swing up your uvula to prevent the food making a dash for freedom up your nose. On second thoughts don't worry about doing this – it happens automatically.

• NOTE 1: Try not to laugh when you eat. When you laugh your uvula swings DOWN – so you could find that the soup you've just slurped up is dribbling out of your nostrils!

• NOTE 2: Try not to breathe whilst you're swallowing. If you do your food goes down your windpipe and you have to cough it up! You've got a little lid called the epiglottis (eppy-glot-tis) that closes off the top of your windpipe to prevent this happening.

Wouldn't you like to know what really happens to your food after you swallow it? No? Go on – it's REALLY horrible.

A gruesome guts tour

Here's a gruesomely thrilling alternative to the usual boring tourist trip. Just imagine being shrunk down to the size of a pinhead and boarding a coach the size of a pea. Then imagine going on a guided tour of someone else's guts! And guess what? Your dinner's thrown in! That's if you feel like eating any . . .

The Horrible Holiday Company proudly present...

THE GRUESOME GUTS GETAWAY!

EMBARK ON THE TRIP OF A LUNCHTIME.

THE SMALL PRINT

1. If you get digested and turned into a chemical soup it's not our fault – OK?

2. There will be <u>no</u> toilet stops until the end of the tour.

1.00 pm Enter the mouth. Fasten your safety belts and close the windows securely. It's wet outside and we're about to dive down the gullet waterfall. Splosh!

GRUESOME GUTS TOURS

1.01 pm
Amazing 9 to
13-second free-fall
as we're squeezed
25cm (10 inches)
down the gullet!

1.02-6 pm Five hour stopover in the stomach. Plenty of time to admire the slimy stomach walls with their 35 million digestive juice-producing pits.

▶ Enjoy the beautiful sunset effect as a red hot pepper makes the stomach glow.

▶ Listen to the mighty roar of the rumbling stomach as trapped gases squelch around amongst the food.

▶ Experience the gut-churning thrill of the stomach big dipper as it churns and churns again every 20 seconds. (If you feel a bit queasy, sick-bags are provided.)

6.00 pm A sudden lurch takes us from the stomach into the intestine. Then what better than a relaxing 6m (6.5 yards) cruise down the scenic small intestine? (Speed 2.5cm (1 inch) per minute.)

► Feel the lovely smooth gliding motion as we're squeezed along. The slimy gut walls help to stop the guts from digesting themselves.

► Marvel at the velvety insides of the intestines made up of five million tiny projections called villi.

► Gasp as we are covered in enzyme-rich digestive juices squirting down from the pancreas and liver.

► Wonder as the food chemicals are sucked into the villi.

► Puzzle over the mystery of the appendix. Everyone's got one of these finger-like things sticking out of their intestines. But no-one knows what it's for!

10.00 pm Spend the night in the comfortable and spacious large intestines. Here the surroundings are peaceful, lie back and listen for the relaxing gurgling of the water as it's taken out of the remains of the food and back into the body.

7.30 am (Give or take a few hours). Put on your life jacket and parachute. It's time for splash down in the toilet!

Some sickening scientists

Of course, the first scientists who investigated the guts had to learn the hard way. That's by gruesome guesswork, sickening speculation and some awful emetic* experiments.

* WARNING TO READERS: An emetic is something that makes you throw up. Vomiting is a reflex action caused by strong squeezing of the muscles around the stomach. It could even be triggered by reading this chapter. Don't try any of these experiments at home – or at school!

Emetic experiments

If you thought that science is all about spotless white coats and squeaky-clean labs . . . THINK AGAIN! Here are some sickening experiments you shouldn't try.

1 René Réamur (1683-1757)

Claim to fame: Famous French scientist. Expert on just about everything, including technology and industry.

Emetic experiment: Trained a kite – (that's a bird not the thing on a string) to sick up its food. Then he pored over the vile vomit to see what the half-digested food looked like.

Disgusting discovery: The meat didn't go rotten inside the bird's guts. This was because the chemicals in the bird's stomach killed the germs that made things rot.

MUST BE THAT RABBIT I CAUGHT LAST NIGHT!

2 Lazzaro Spallanzani (1729-1799)

Claim to fame: Famous Italian scientist. Expert on volcanoes, electric fish, thunderclouds and how a snail grows its head back after you cut it off.

Revolting research included:

● Forcing animals to swallow food in tubes or tied to string and then making them sick up the food so he could study how the food had changed. The animals included cats, dogs, oxen, newts, sheep, a horse and some sinister-looking snakes.

○ Doing the same experiment on himself. Eating his own sicked-up food. He ate one bit of food three times just to see how it had changed!

○ Making himself sick again so that he could study his own stomach juices.

Emetic experiment: Kept a container of sick in a warm place for a few hours.

Disgusting discovery: The food continued to be digested. (This was because the enzymes produced by the stomach didn't stop working.)

OH DEAR — IT MUST HAVE BEEN SOMETHING YOU ATE!

3 Claude Bernard (1813-1878)

Claim to fame: French scientist. Cut up loads of human bodies and made disgusting discoveries about blood and nerves.

Revolting research: Kidnapped dogs (or should this be "dognapped"?) for his experiments. Poked tubes into the poor pooches' stomachs to find out what was going on.

Emetic experiment: Added juice from a dog's pancreas to fatty foods.

Disgusting discovery: The fats were digested and made a greasy mess. (This was because digestive juices produced by the pancreas digest fats.)

Could you perform experiments like these? Would you want to? If your answer is "YUGGGHHH!" or "WHICH WAY TO THE BATHROOM?!" then you don't have the stomach for the job. So you wouldn't want to be at Fort Mackinac, United States in 1822...

The stomach for the job

The young man moaned in agony. A carelessly loaded shotgun had exploded – blasting a 15 cm (6 inch) hole in Alexis St. Martin's side ... you could see all his insides. The young Canadian hunter had two broken ribs, a damaged lung and ... a hole in his stomach.

HMM, CHOCCYFLAKES FOR BREAKFAST I SEE!

Dr William Beaumont looked at these injuries and shook his head sadly. The patient would die soon. Very soon. In those days the only treatment for this type of wound was to slap on a bandage and arrange the funeral. But against all expectations, Alexis survived the night. Weeks became months and the young man even started to get better! But he had an embarrassing problem.

The stomach hole refused to heal. So whenever he felt peckish Alexis had to bandage his tum to stop its gruesome contents from slopping out!

Oddly enough the young man cheerfully put up with this appalling arrangement. So the devious doctor seized the opportunity to perform some gruesome gut experiments. One day he asked Alexis to swallow a bit of raw meat on a thread. Later he pulled it up again to see how it had changed. On another occasion Dr Beaumont poked a thermometer through the hole and watched it leap about as the stomach churned!

The doctor soon discovered that stomach juice is produced in large amounts when there's food in the stomach. So he drained some of Alexis's stomach juice out through a pipe and tried to identify the chemicals it contained. First of all he tasted it – YUCK! But as he wasn't sure what it was he sent it to some scientist friends.

They discovered the juice contained hydrochloric acid –
a powerful dissolving chemical. This is useful for
breaking down food and killing germs.

Sometimes the doctor and his patient would have a
row. You've got to see it from Alexis' point of view. For
two years Dr Beaumont had nursed him. But on the other
hand . . . well, if there's one thing worse than having a
hole in your body – it's being chased around by a
meddlesome medic trying to terrorise your tummy. And
over the next few years Dr Beaumont took to following
Alexis so he could perform even more horrible
experiments!

Oddly enough these shouting matches provided Dr
Beaumont with yet more sickening scientific data. He
couldn't help noticing that when Alexis got cross, his
stomach went all red and quivery!

At last in 1833 Dr Beaumont published his findings. It
had taken 11 years of tests and tantrums. Packed full of
stomach-churning pictures, the book was an overnight
success. The doctor achieved fame and fortune. Yet he
owed his entire achievement to one gruesome fact . . .
he'd had the stomach for the job!

A weighty matter

Three hundred years ago an Italian scientist named Santorio Santorio decided to build an incredible weighing machine. It swung from the ceiling and was big enough for his chair, desk and bed! There was even room for his prized silver chamber pot. Every day Santorio sat in the machine and recorded his weight.

For 30 years he weighed himself. He weighed himself before meals, after meals and during meals. He even weighed all his waste products.

But he still couldn't figure it out. Why did his food weigh more than the contents of his silver chamber pot?

Here's the answer. Much of the missing food turns into energy to power the body. Digested food molecules go from the guts to the blood and then off to feed billions of hungry body cells. Spare sugar and fats get carted off by a useful blood vessel to the storage place in the liver.

Liver fact file

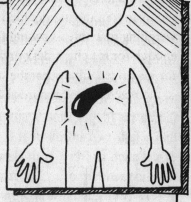

Name of body part: Liver

Where found: On top of the guts and under the diaphragm.

Useful things it does: What doesn't it do? (See below.)

Grisly details: If the liver doesn't work, waste body products build up in the skin.

Amazing features: You can lose 90 per cent of your liver and survive. That little bit of liver grows into a lovely new liver!

The lively liver

Yes – your liver certainly has a good time – scientists know of 500 jobs it tackles. There may be even more that haven't yet been discovered! The liver. . .

• Controls the amount of sugar in the blood. This is done with the aid of a substance called insulin produced by the pancreas. Too little insulin causes a disease called diabetes.

• Stores spare fat and carbohydrates.

• Makes Vitamin A.

• Gets rid of old red blood cells.

• Produces digestive juices.

• Keeps you warm – all these activities produce heat!

But not all your food is used by the body. Some of it just isn't needed – so the body chucks it out!

Gruesome garbage disposal 1 – waste food

1 Every day some of your food puts in a reappearance. It's stained brown by the liver's digestive juices – lovely.

2 This waste food is called faeces – that's Latin for "dregs" – which just about sums it up.

3 Children produce 65-171g (2-6 ounces) of the stuff every day. Some fearless scientists have discovered that faeces is 75 per cent water, and of the solid material that's left, two thirds of it is food that your body can't digest such as fibre, fruit skins and seeds. And the other third is made up of . . . germs!

4 Yes! Your guts swarm with billions of germs that have somehow managed to get past the acid in the stomach. Ugh! Fortunately, few of them do much harm.

5 UNFORTUNATELY, they do produce gases which, added to the gases from food and drink, can reappear at either end of the body – with hilarious or embarrassing but always noisy (and sometimes smelly) results.

6 But the really bad news is that these gases include methane, a chemical that burns easily. (NOTE: please don't experiment on yourself or your teacher to prove this. One surgeon cut open a man's guts and caused a gas explosion!)

Gruesome garbage disposal 2 – waste water

Much of your food is made up of water. Cucumbers, for example, are 90 per cent water and ten per cent vegetable. Your body is over two-thirds water and water is very useful for making lots of gruesome body fluids such as tears, runny snot and digestive juices. But spare water just isn't needed so it's filtered out by your kidneys.

Kidneys fact file

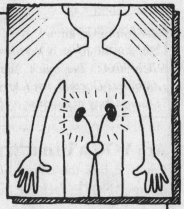

Name of body part: Kidneys

Where found: You've got two at the back of your body just below your lowest ribs.

Useful things it does: Remove spare water, unwanted salt and waste chemicals from the blood.

Grisly details: If not enough water passes through the kidneys the waste forms agonisingly painful stones.

Amazing features: Your kidneys filter over 1,500 litres (330 gallons) of blood every day.

How the kidneys work

The kidneys are like millions of tiny coffee filters linked

up to a drainpipe.

1 Each filter takes the form of a tiny tube.

2 A little capsule at the start of each tube takes in fluid from the blood.

3 As the fluid runs down the tube, all the really useful stuff such as molecules of food escape back into the blood.

4 All the useless unwanted water plus any extra salts and poisonous wastes trickle down the drainpipe into the bladder.

5 This watery waste is urine.

Bet you never knew!
You can discover a person's state of health by studying their urine. Too much sugar in the urine is a sign of diabetes. Doctors used to taste urine to discover this! Disease may also cause a change in the colour of urine.

Are YOU a Urine Expert?

Can you link the colour of these urine samples to the disease? NOTE: feel free to colour in the urine yourself!

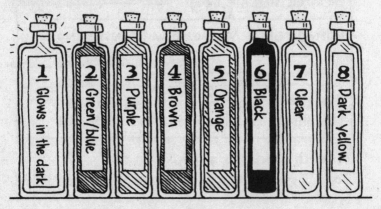

1| Glows in the dark
2| Green/blue
3| Purple
4| Brown
5| Orange
6| Black
7| Clear
8| Dark yellow

Cause of the colour. . .

a) The patient has been injected with blood from an animal.

b) Blackwater fever – a nasty tropical disease.

c) The patient has been eating too many food colourings.

d) The patient has been drinking a lot of liquid.

e) The patient has been eating too much beetroot or blackberries.

f) The patient is feverish and has lost a lot of water by sweating.

g) The patient has been eating too many carrots.

h) The patient is a space monster.

Answers: 1 h) 2 c) 3 e) 4 b) 5 g) 6 a) 7 d) 8 f)

Of course, your kidneys couldn't work if your blood wasn't doing its job. That's rushing round your body as fast as your heaving heart can pump it out! Warning. If the sight of buckets of blood makes you wobble at the knees it's wise to put on a blindfold before reading the next chapter.

THE BL**OO**DY BITS

You may think that EVERYTHING to do with the body is blood-curdling. But some bits are bloodier than others. Take, for example, blood itself and the heart that keeps it moving. But blood is also vital for life – here's why. . .

Blood fact file

Name of body part: Blood

Where found: Throughout the body in a network of blood vessels. You've got about five litres of the red stuff.

Useful things it does: Delivers food and oxygen and other useful things your cells need to keep going.

Grisly details: You can lose one third of your blood without harm. But if you lose half – it's FATAL!

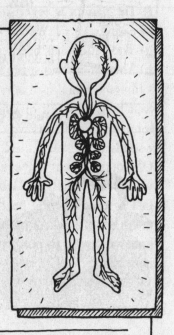

Amazing features: Blood is so full of things that it's amazing they all fit in – see below.

Blood – what's in it for me?

1 Your blood is yellow! Yes, it's true. If you leave a test tube full of blood for a few hours the blood cells sink to the bottom and you're left with a clear yellow fluid.

2 The yellow stuff is called plasma – it's 90 per cent water and 10 per cent chemicals such as those tasty molecules and minerals that your cells need to grow and stay healthy. Scientists have discovered how to dry plasma to a powder and turn it back into a liquid by adding water.

3 Imagine blood as a sort of hot soup squirting through your body. It's full of sugars and other molecules from your food – which is why vampires and mosquitoes find it so tasty.

4 Blood is thicker than water. In fact, it's THREE TIMES thicker. That's not surprising considering that blood is swarming with cells . . . here's what you get in one teeny little millimetre-sized drop!

- 7,000 white blood cells
- 300,000 platelets – (these are little bits of bone-marrow cell that help your blood to clot).

- 5 million red blood cells

Impressive isn't it? But that's nothing. . .

5 In all, your body contains. . .

- 35,000,000,000 (35,000 million) white cells,
- 500,000,000,000 (500,000 million) platelets and
- 25,000,000,000,000 (25 trillion) red blood cells.

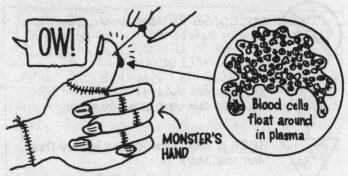

Or so the scientists say. . .

6 But this is only guess-work because it's impossible to count all those cells.

7 The problem isn't just the huge numbers. Every second, three million new red blood cells are made in your bone marrow and three million others die. So by the time you've finally finished counting – you've got to start all over again!

8 There's plenty of room for all these blood cells. Your body contains about 96,558 km (59,962 miles) of blood vessels. If you took someone's blood vessels and laid them end to end they'd go twice round the world. Just imagine a motorway like that!

But if you want to zoom along the blood superhighway in your very own nippy little red blood cell you'll have to learn the rules of the road.

The blood Highway Code

RULE 1: Understand the one way system. Arteries go <u>AWAY</u> from the heart and veins go <u>TOWARDS</u> the heart. <u>NOT THE OTHER WAY ROUND!</u>

RULE 2: No "U" turns allowed. Valves in the veins form bottle necks that stop you reversing.

RULE 3: Red blood cells travel in the centre and white cells creep along the edges.

RULE 4: Make sure you can identify these other road users.

RED BLOOD CELLS   WHITE BLOOD CELLS   PLATELETS

RULE 5: Make sure you don't go over the speed limits. In the big arteries over the heart it's one metre every two seconds. In the capillaries – that's the very tiny blood vessels – it's one metre every half-an-hour!

RULE 6: After four months all the red blood cells must report to the liver scrap yard to be broken up. All platelets to be broken up after two weeks.

RULE 7: Beware of blood clots around wounds! All the platelets stick together and produce chemicals that make the plasma sticky. Other road users steer clear – unless you're a real clot!

If you ever get a bit short of blood you might need a blood transfusion. That's when you're given someone else's blood instead of your own. Luckily you don't have to give it back.

A blood-curdling story

Three centuries ago scientists began to wonder whether it was possible to inject blood into humans. But would it work? There was only one way to find out!

One day in 1667 an audience of top British scientists gathered to watch a terrifying trial transfusion. At the centre of attention was a man who had bravely volunteered to have an extra 340 g (12 ounces) of blood injected into his veins. The red stuff had been kindly donated by – a sheep!

1 Can you guess what happened?

a) The volunteer survived.

b) The volunteer's hair turned woolly and he died.

c) The volunteer went mad.

Answer: c) He was described as a bit "cracked in the head". But the scientists reckoned the test worth repeating and more blood transfusions were performed.

But then disaster struck. A man died after another blood transfusion in France. No one knew why! The doctor who performed the operation was accused of murder and although he was found not guilty, the French government banned all transfusions.

Meanwhile the Brits carried on. In those days the technology was rather primitive. One day a doctor offered a sick old man the chance of a blood transfusion. Here's what the doctor planned to do. . .

- Fix a silver pipe to each end of a length of chicken gut.
- Wash the chicken gut out with warm water.
- Stick one silver pipe in the arm of a healthy volunteer.
- Stick the other pipe in the old man's veins.
- Allow the blood to flow into the old man.

CHICKEN GUT

SILVER PIPE

2 What do you think happened next?

a) The old man said "YUCK – NOT ON YOUR LIFE!" and died soon afterwards.

b) The old man said "YES" but the transfusion bumped him off.

c) The old man said "YES" – he got better but the volunteer died!

Answer: a)

During a transfusion there was a risk of blood clots forming and blocking vital blood vessels. But what

117

caused these killer clots? The answer emerged in 1900 when Austrian scientist, Karl Landsteiner, discovered that blood was divided into groups. Your blood group depends on the type of chemicals carried by your red blood cells. When red blood cells from different blood groups collide they mistake one another for germs! Germ-zapping chemicals on the outside of each cell zip into action and the cells end up glued together.

Nowadays blood can be stored in a blood bank until it's needed by someone with the same group. Blood banks don't save money but they do save lives. But sadly Karl's was not one of them. In 1943 he died of a heart attack caused by . . . a blood clot.

Oddly enough, whilst some doctors were trying to give their patients extra blood, others were trying to take it away again. These doctors thought that too much blood was bad for you.

Blood-thirsty bleeders

Yes – 200 years ago your local friendly doctor would do more than give you nasty cough medicine! He'd also try to open your veins to remove all that nasty bad blood! In those days doctors had a selection of vicious-looking knives especially designed for this gruesome job.

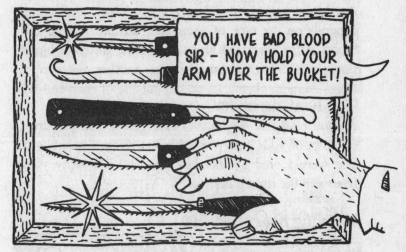

So you don't like the look of them? Well, don't worry – you do have another choice. Can you guess what it is?

A rotten riddle

What's green and yellow and dripping with slime, got ten stomachs, has three stabbing teeth at the front end and by the time it's finished with you it's 15 cm (6 inches) long and GORGED WITH ALL YOUR BLOOD?!

Answer: It's a LOATHSOME leech!!!

And here's the really BAD news! Surgeons were particularly keen on using leeches to take blood from children. They reckoned it was kinder than cutting the kids with the knives!

The heaving heart

As you read this – whatever else you're doing, there's one part of your body that's hard at work. Especially if you were scared by that last bit. Yes, it's lucky your heart's in the right place.

Heaving heart fact file

Name of body part: Heart

Where found: The top of your heart is about 8cm (3 inches) to the left of your breast bone.

Useful things it does: Keeps your blood moving.

Grisly details: Your heart isn't heart-shaped – it's blob-shaped with a tangle of blood vessels on top. It's about 12cm (5 inches) high and weighs 250–300g (9–10 ounces).

Amazing features: It's horribly hard-working (see opposite page).

The horribly hard-working heart

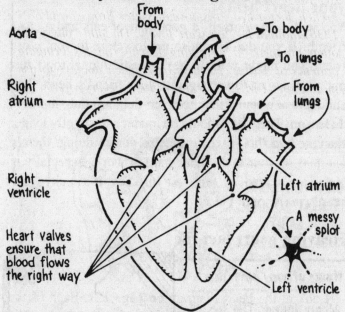

Aorta

From body

To body

To lungs

From lungs

Right atrium

Right ventricle

Heart valves ensure that blood flows the right way

Left atrium

A messy splot

Left ventricle

• Your heart is strong enough to pump blood round your body in one minute.

• Its speed is controlled by the brain and influenced by your feelings – this is why your heart beats faster before a science test. But the heart itself is powered by a built-in pacemaker that triggers the heartbeat with tiny electric shocks. So it's got to keep going!

• In just one day your heart pumps enough blood to fill a 10,000 litre (2,200 gallon) tanker.

• In an average lifetime it beats 3,000,000,000 times.

• And pumps over 300 million litres of blood. That's enough to fill 5,500 large swimming pools!

• And in all that time your heart doesn't stop once, not even when you're asleep.

Dare you find out for yourself . . . how your heart beats?

You will need yourself, a good pair of ears and a close friend. (If you don't want to get too close to your close friend you might want to get a plastic funnel too.) Just put your ear or funnel against your friend's heart. You should hear a sound that goes lup-dub, lup-dub, lup-dub, and so on. The "lup" should be louder and slightly longer than the "dub".

CAN YOU MAKE IT BEAT LOUDER PLEASE?

Look at the heart diagram on page 121. Each of the four chambers pumps blood in the direction shown. The "lup" sound is the valves at the opening of the ventricles slamming shut. Then the ventricles squeeze the blood out and the "dub" sound you can hear is the closing of the heart valves to prevent the blood squirting backwards.

Your heart isn't the only part of your body that beats. You can feel the blood pulsing in places such as the side of your wrist just under your thumb and on the sides of your neck. What causes these pulses?

a) The arteries pumping the blood forward.

b) The arteries bulging out as a surge of blood from the heart passes by.

c) A bulge in the veins caused by the blood stopping for a moment.

You might wonder why half your heart is squirting blood to your lungs. Well, your lungs are more than a couple of wheezy wind-bags. They're needed to supply your body with oxygen and the blood takes the oxygen round your body. And without this gas you'd be gasping!

THE GASPING LUNGS

You need your lungs like a breath of fresh air. Literally. Day after day, year after year, your lungs keep puffing away – about 600 million puffs in a lifetime. And you never need to remind them to do their job. But it's a difficult job and the facts that follow about breathing will leave you gasping.

Gasping lungs fact file

Name of body part: Lungs

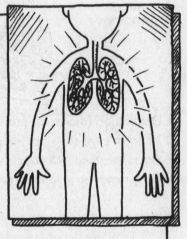

Where found: In the chest on either side of the heart. The heart fits into a snug little hollow against the left lung.

Useful things they do: Breathe in air so that oxygen can get into your blood and supply your cells.

Grisly details: Once smokers get ash into their lungs they NEVER get it out again. Heavy smokers' lungs end up like tacky old tar buckets.

Amazing features: Your lungs contain 750 million little tubes and capsules. If these were laid out flat they could cover a tennis court.

Breathing: the inside story

"As easy as breathing" – or so they say. But in fact there's nothing easy about breathing. Here's what happens when you try.

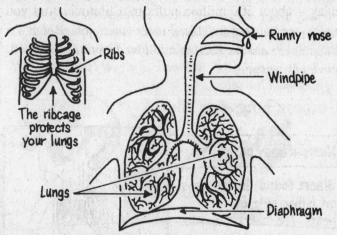

Runny nose

Ribs

Windpipe

The ribcage protects your lungs

Lungs

Diaphragm

1 Diaphragm (dia-fram) pulls down.

2 Your rib cage rises up.

3 Air is breathed in through your nose and mouth.

4 The air ends up in little capsules called alveoli (al-ve-ol-i).

Your breathing space

The alveoli are the places where breathing actually takes place. Oxygen gas from the air passes into the blood and hops aboard red blood cells for a free ride round the body. Meanwhile the carbon dioxide gas (produced as a waste product by your cells and dissolved in the blood) is rushing the other way. All this takes just one third of a second. Then, the breathing steps 1-4 go into reverse as the air is puffed out again. Yes, it all happens with breathless speed.

Have you got blue blood in your veins? When red blood cells take oxygen from the lungs they're bright red. But after the cells give up their oxygen they're dark red. This is why you get dark red blood in veins returning to the heart. If you're fair-skinned these veins appear blue! It was once said the nobility had blue blood. They stayed indoors so their skin was pale and you could see their gruesome blue veins!

WHO'S FAKING THEIR NOBILITY?

Test your teacher

Is your teacher full of hot air? This tricky test will leave him or her breathless. Here's a clue to start him or her off. An adult breathes about six litres of air a minute.

1 A man stands in a telephone box to make a phone call. The telephone box contains about 270 litres (59 gallons) of air and once the door is closed no more air can get in. How long can the man speak on the phone before he faints from lack of air?

a) 45 minutes

b) 4 hours

c) 45 hours

2 A woman goes to sleep in a room 1.8 x 1.8 x 1.5 metres (2 x 2 x 1.5 yards). The room contains about 1,300 litres (286 gallons) of air. Would she have enough air to survive the night? (Clue: you only need about half the normal amount of air when you're asleep.)

a) Yes – and the following day too!

b) No – she'd die of suffocation.

c) Yes – just about!

3 Think about the size of the room in question 2. How much air do you need to last a lifetime?

a) Enough to fill two large airships.

b) Enough to fill a small hot-air balloon.

c) Enough to fill 339,174 hot-air balloons.

4 Why would someone die if they tried to hide in a lake and breathe through a hollow reed?

a) The lungs can't work in very cold water.

b) The water pressing against the body stops the lungs from breathing out.

c) The water gets in though the ears and drowning follows.

5 A woman has an attack of hiccuping. What part of her breathing equipment is making her hiccup?

a) Her diaphragm

b) Her ribs

c) Her lungs

127

Horrible hiccups

What do you think caused this dramatic cure?

a) A massive electric shock

b) A faith healer

c) She had an operation

Dare you find out for yourself . . . how you talk?

TALKING. Some people never seem to stop. This sad affliction is particularly common amongst teachers. Naturally YOU know how to talk (and when to stop). But can you say what part your lungs play?

Half-way up your windpipe is a triangular opening. It's behind the little bump in your throat that some people call the "Adam's apple". On two sides of this opening, folds of skin stretch as you speak and wobble as air puffs past from the lungs. They're your vocal chords. The larger the chords, the deeper the sounds you can make (this is why most children have squeaky voices).

The basic sounds produced by your vibrating vocal chords are altered by the position of your tongue, lower lip and jaw. You can see how important these bits are when you try this unspeakable speech challenge.

1 Say the word "she" whilst keeping your tongue in your cheek (so you can't move it!).

2 Say the word "pie" without your lips touching one another.

3 Put your hand under your chin and try to talk without your lower jaw moving down.

Which of the above were. . .
a) Possible
b) Just possible but it sounded funny.
c) Impossible
Enjoy endless fun watching your friends attempt the same challenge!

Answers: 1 b) 2 c) 3 b)

Gasping lungs sound-effects

Here are a few other sounds your gasping lungs can make. . .

Yawning

This happens when not enough air is getting to your lungs. So you suddenly take a deep gulp of air. It can also be triggered by boring science lessons.

Laughing

This happens when deep breaths, caused by movements of the diaphragm, are followed by a few short puffs of air from your lungs. This can be triggered by watching your teacher fall off his bicycle.

HA HA HA
HEE HEE
HO HO HO

YOU CAN STAY BEHIND AND MEND MY BIKE WATKINS!

Crying

Your breathing is exactly the same as when you laugh. Only your feelings are different. Crying may occur as a direct result of having laughed at the wrong moment.

But whatever you do with your lungs there is something you ought to know first. And it's no laughing matter . . . here's the bad news.

Breathing is bad for you

The air you breathe isn't always as pure as it could be. Especially if you live in a big city. Yes – every day you breathe in 20,000,000,000 (20,000 million) tiny bits of pollution, dust and dirt! THE GOOD NEWS . . . your body has ways of dealing with unwelcome visitors.

1 Inside your nose, windpipe and lung tubes there are tiny hairs called cilia (silly-er). Their job is to waft all that nasty stuff back into your mouth and nostrils.

2 The snot in your nose and windpipe is a deadly dust trap. Once stuck in the snot there's no escape for the

grimy gatecrashers. Have you ever noticed that when you work in a dirty place your snot turns black?!

The better news

You can actually cough up dirt . . . this involves closing the top of your windpipe and then suddenly releasing it to allow a blast of puff out at the speed of 150 metres (164 yards) a second!

And sneeze out snot. . . Something tickles the inside of your nose. You close and then open your throat. The air trapped in your lungs blasts its way out. Your tongue blocks the way into your mouth so the dirty, snotty mini-hurricane shoots out of your nose at over 160 km (99 miles) an hour!

ATCHOOOOOO!

The really bad news

It's not just dirt and debris that make you cough and sneeze. The air we breathe is laden with billions and billions of germs. And their whole aim in life is to invade your body and cause disgusting diseases! Atishoooooooo!

YES, THE NEXT CHAPTER IS DEAD INTERESTING . . .

DEADLY DISEASES

Remember that sneeze at the end of the previous chapter? It was more than just a puff of air. It was a million droplets of snotty spit and countless germs zooming through the air in search of a victim. And causing disgusting or even deadly diseases. So welcome to the war zone right inside your body! Amazingly, most of the time you don't even know a war's going on!

Little monsters

There are thousands of different types of germs but they fall into two main groups. The brutal bacteria and the vicious viruses – but they're all little monsters.

Brutal bacteria

Bacteria come in a variety of sinister shapes and sizes. Some look like octopuses, others are like sausages and others still have little whip-like tails so they can swim around. They double their numbers every 20 minutes and increase their numbers eight times in one hour. In eight hours a single bacterium can make 16 million copies of itself!

There's something nasty in the garden shed. Something dark and invisible hiding in the corners of your school. And it's waiting to pounce. Many bacteria lurk in shadows because they're destroyed by sunlight. In gloomy weather they float on the wind as high as the clouds. And some are armed with poisonous toxins 100,000 times more powerful than the deadly poison strychnine!

Rogue's gallery

The brutal bacteria include microbes that cause boils, tetanus and upset stomachs. Vicious viruses include colds, chickenpox and measles. There are hundreds of other disease-causing germs – these are just a few of the more sinister specimens!

Botulinus (Bot-tu-line-us)

HABITS: Lurks in half-cooked potted meat, soil and rotting leaves.

DAMAGE REPORT: Deadly toxins. Cause double vision, sickness and death!

KNOWN CRIMES: Killed eight fishermen in Scotland in 1922. They had all eaten botulinus-infected sandwiches.

DANGER RATING: Deadly. It makes school dinners look healthy. (But don't worry, this disease is extremely rare!)

Leprosy

HABITS: You can only catch it from prolonged contact with people who already have the disease (and not everyone with leprosy has the catching sort anyway). Slow to develop. It can take years but in the worst cases it makes fingers and toes drop off.

DAMAGE REPORT: Attacks the nerves and skin.

KNOWN CRIMES: Affects several million people in hot countries.

DANGER RATING: Not so dangerous because it's difficult to catch - but very, very nasty if you've got it!

Vicious viruses

To a virus one of your body cells looks like a little planet. That's not surprising because viruses are thousands of times smaller even than bacteria. The virus touches down onto a body cell like a spacecraft landing on the moon. Then the vicious virus injects chemicals to make the cell produce hundreds more viruses. Within half-an-hour all the viruses fly off to seek more victims and the poor old cell splits like a pea pod. It's died from over-work!

Influenza

HABITS: Changes its form every year so your body's defences can't recognise it easily.

DAMAGE REPORT: Fever, aches and pains, runny nose – a few days off school.

KNOWN CRIMES: In 1918 a world-wide 'flu epidemic killed 25 million people.

DANGER RATING: No known cure. Luckily most types of influenza don't kill you – otherwise you'd need more than a few days off school.

Typhus

HABITS: Lives inside lice that scratch their disgusting droppings into the human skin. Ugh!

DAMAGE REPORT: Causes a red rash, fever and death. Kills the louse too by the way – but who cares?

KNOWN CRIMES: Unlike most criminals, typhus germs actually enjoy prison. In 1750 infected lice jumped from criminals to the judges and jurors at a London trial. Three judges and eight jurymen suffered the death penalty.

DANGER RATING: Still common in many parts of the world but can be treated by drugs.

The body strikes back

Now for the good news. Your body is ready and waiting to bash germs – even if you're not! As part of its defences your body makes lots of germ-killing chemicals. How was this discovered? Well, the story's a bit of a weepie.

A tearful story

1. In 1921, scientist Alexander Fleming was breeding germs for an experiment. He had a bad cold. A drop of snot splashed the germs and they all died!

ATCHOO

SNOT

2. Fleming realised that snot must contain a germ-killing chemical. He experimented using blood plasma, spit and tears.

I DON'T THINK HE LIKES US!

SPIT

SPIT

3. Tears were good germ killers. To get more, Fleming ambushed visitors to his lab and squirted lemon juice in their eyes! (Don't try this – it stings!)

4. He even picked on small children. (He paid them afterwards.)

5. Further experiments proved that egg-white also killed germs. So Fleming started breaking eggs.

6. Then he discovered that fish eggs killed germs too. So he went fishing – oddly enough this was his hobby!

A rotten result

In 1965 scientists found that the germ-killing substance was an enzyme called lysozyme (lie-so-zime). It's found in all the things that Fleming tested. That's the good news. But sadly, lysozyme doesn't kill all known germs – just a few of them.

Luckily you've got a built-in army to defend you from germs. Every day they fight and die on your behalf. Recognise them? They're your wonderful white blood cells – all 35,000,000,000 (35,000 million) of them! Here's what they do.

Immune system fact file

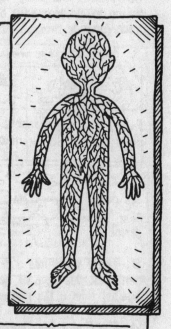

Name of body part: The immune system

Where found: A network of drainage tubes called the lymph system. Also includes your white blood cells.

Useful things they do: Fight germs and keep you healthy.

Grisly details: Pus from an infected wound consists of millions of white blood cells that have been done to death by germs.

Amazing features: White blood cells "talk" to one another using chemical substances that pass on messages such as, "Bash that virus!"

1 The tubes form a drainage system for lymph – a watery fluid that dribbles from the blood vessels.
2 Nodes: These grape-sized little lumps filter out nasty

germs from the tubes. They swell up and get bigger when you're sick.

3 Spleen: Helps make white blood cells in babies.

4 Thymus makes some white blood cells.

Your battling body

Here's how your body fights back. Germs are always trying to get into your body – through your nose, in your food or through cuts and scratches.

1. But your brave white blood cells are ready . . .

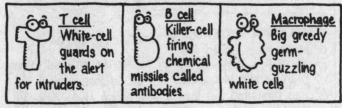

T cell
White-cell guards on the alert for intruders.

B cell
Killer-cell firing chemical missiles called antibodies.

Macrophage
Big greedy germ-guzzling white cells

2. The T cell grabs a wriggling germ!

3. The T cell finds a B cell that makes antibodies that can stick this type of germ together. It's a desperate race against time – the germs are breeding fast!

4. The B cell fires antibodies to gum the germs together.

5. The T cell orders the B cell to make loads of copies of itself to attack any other germs loitering nearby.

6. The macrophage flows round the stuck-up germs. Reaches out long jelly-like arms to encircle them. Then it gobbles the germs! It can grab and guzzle 20 bacteria at a time and dissolve them whilst they're still alive! Congratulations, you win!

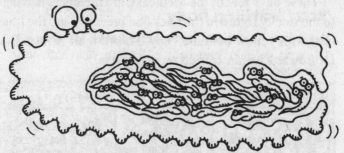

You've won if you destroy all the germs without losing too many white blood cells. It's OK to lose a few hundred thousand but lose a few billion and you're in trouble! Meanwhile bits of half-digested bacteria are left lying around on the battlefield.

How to be incredibly immune

Once you've had a certain illness, you needn't worry about getting it again – ever. Some of your white blood cells store the information about how to make the antibodies. This way, your body can store details of an incredible 18 billion types of antibody.

But sometimes your immune system needs a boost. That's why you need nasty injections. When you have a jab you are being injected with dead germs. YUCK!

These allow your body to make the antibodies needed to fight the actual full-blown disease. Yuck! This painful process is called vaccination. Here's how the modern form of vaccination was developed in 1796.

Just the jab

Some of the audience yawned rudely or snorted angrily. One muttered under his breath, "That Jenner's going on about cowpox again!"

These days few of the Medical Club members listened to the stocky figure in the buckskin breeches and the blue coat with yellow buttons. They'd heard it all before. But Dr Edward Jenner carried on regardless.

"Smallpox kills millions of people. It causes fever and covers the body with pus-filled spots. People lucky enough to survive are scarred for life. I believe that those who get the milder disease of cowpox are protected from getting smallpox."

"Why don't you experiment?!" someone shouted.

"Yes," yelled another, "On yourself!"

"But," shouted Jenner above the uproar, "many country people also believe it to be true!"

The audience exploded with laughter – they didn't think much of country folk.

Jenner sat back down – humiliated once again. He remembered going to the doctor's as an eight-year-old boy. He was terrified of the physician and the huge needle with its thread dripping with pus from a smallpox victim. This was the traditional form of vaccination using live germs and it was very dangerous. The needle scratch was supposed to cause a mild smallpox and somehow prevent the full-blown disease. But it gave young Jenner such a terrible fever that he nearly died.

There had to be a better way. Jenner was certain that people who got cowpox from milking infected cows never got smallpox. If only he could prove it. . .

One day, a young milkmaid named Sara Nelmes came into the tiny garden hut that Jenner used as his surgery. The girl was in a bad way.

She'd scratched her hand and as the doctor examined her he noticed bluish raised-up spots.

"You have the cowpox, Sara?"

"Yes, sir," the milkmaid blushed. "But at least I won't get the smallpox."

Jenner smiled. "Sara, with your permission I would like to perform a small experiment."

With a needle Dr Jenner took a drop of pus from Sara's hand and then. . . This was the moment for which he had waited for over 20 years. He decided to inject the pus into an eight-year-old boy named James Phipps. Then Jenner saw the fear in the child's eyes and remembered his own terror of the doctor with the huge needle.

IT'S ALL IN THE NAME OF SCIENCE JAMES!

So Jenner closed his eyes and gritted his teeth as he made two scratches on the boy's arm. In the next few days James would suffer the sores and discomfort of cowpox. But would this be enough to ward off the more deadly threat of smallpox?

Six weeks later Jenner held his breath as he scratched poor James again – this time with pus from a smallpox victim. Now came the real test. There would be a two week pause and then . . . what? Perhaps the boy would suffer crippling backaches, the fever and shivering and the deadly killer spots. Supposing Jenner was wrong . . . the child might even die. And then the doctor would face the death penalty for murdering his young patient!

But weeks passed and James remained healthy. The child was now immune to smallpox. Some people still jeered. They sang songs about people turning into cows after a cowpox injection.

"On their foreheads, o horrible crumpled horns bud;
Tom with his tail, and poor William all hairy . . ."

But Dr Jenner soon hit back with a book packed with tasteful colour pictures of pus-filled cowpox blisters. More physicians backed the doctor and soon richer people began to ask for the treatment. It proved to be "just the jab" for beating smallpox. Dr Jenner grew rich and successful but he never forgot the boy who had made it possible. What did he give James as a thank-you present?

a) His very own thatched cottage with flowers round the door.

b) A needle made from solid gold.

c) One shilling (that's equivalent to 5p).

Answer: a)

Smallpox smashed

The virus that caused smallpox was living on borrowed time. Throughout Europe and North America governments began to organise vaccination programmes. By 1980 a determined world-wide campaign of vaccination led to a historic announcement from the World Health Organisation . . . smallpox had been wiped off the face of the Earth. Meanwhile, scientists had discovered vaccines for many more diseases. In 1994 all British kids were given measles jabs. Ouch!

But even if you manage to remain healthy your body never stays the same. There's always something going on even if it's a bit of a pain. Oh well – it's all part of growing up.

GROWING PAINS

You might not always like your body – but it'll grow on you. You were growing even before you were born and you spend your first 20 years getting bigger. Growing is a bit of a pain for your parents because you always need new clothes and shoes. But after you stop growing you start ageing – and that's even more of a pain!

Relatively painful

Some of the biggest growing pains are caused by stupid comments from your relatives. Every Christmas they burst into your home to inspect you from head to toe and exclaim, "Haven't you grown!" At this point the best thing to do is look rather sad and say...

HAVEN'T YOU SHRUNK?

On second thoughts – better keep quiet or you won't get any presents. Here are a few things you need to know about growing.

Tall stories

1 You don't grow at the same speed all the time. You grow quickly in your first two years. Then up to the age of ten your growth steadies before speeding up again in your teenage years.

2 As you grow the proportions of your body change. For example, a baby's head takes up about 25 per cent of its length. But in an adult the head is only 12.5 per cent of its body length.

3 It's lucky these things happen otherwise you'd look pretty odd. You wouldn't want a giant-sized head – would you?

But why do people grow? If you asked a scientist this interesting question you wouldn't just get one answer – you'd get two!

1 The fairly simple answer.

2 The excruciatingly complicated but fascinating answer involving large dollops of scientific gobbledy-gook.

So which do you want to hear first?

THE HUMAN STRUCTURE ENLARGES WHEN TRIGGERED BY CHROMOSOMAL AND HORMONAL CHANGES, BLAH, BLAH, BLAH . . .

The fairly simple answer

The speed at which you grow is affected by diet. Eat a normal balanced amount of food and you'll grow taller than if you lived off scraps that the pigs won't eat. (No, I'm not talking about school dinners!) Health is also an important factor. Some bone diseases stop people from growing properly.

The excruciatingly complicated answer. . .

The speed at which you grow is controlled by a hormone produced in your brain. So what exactly is a hormone? I'm afraid you've got to know this before you can begin to understand the excruciatingly complicated answer. . .

Horrible hormones fact file

Name of body part: Hormones

Where found: Made by glands in different parts of the body.

Useful things they do: Cause changes in the body. For example, some hormones give teenagers a grown-up appearance.

Grisly details: Hormones cause horrible problems (see below).

Amazing features: Cortisol (cor-tis-sol), made by the adrenal glands, is a chemical alarm clock that wakes you up!

Where to find your glands. . .

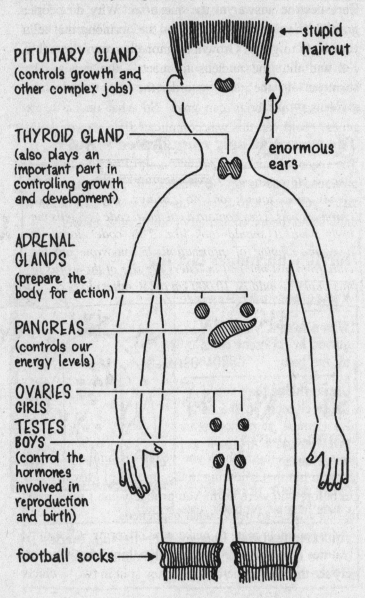

← stupid haircut

PITUITARY GLAND
(controls growth and other complex jobs)

THYROID GLAND
(also plays an important part in controlling growth and development)

enormous ears

ADRENAL GLANDS
(prepare the body for action)

PANCREAS
(controls our energy levels)

OVARIES
GIRLS

TESTES
BOYS
(control the hormones involved in reproduction and birth)

football socks →

Growing and genes

Here lies the answer to the question, "Why do people grow?" The pituitary also makes the hormone that tells your body to grow! Growth hormone burrows through a cell and into the nucleus to meet – the genes. The hormone tells the genes to order the cells to grow and divide so your body can grow. So what on earth are genes? (Told you this was complicated!)

Bet you never knew!
Genes are found on 46 stringy objects called chromosomes. They contain a chemical code that tells the body what it should look like. This code stores an awesome amount of information. If you wrote out the code from just one cell in letters the size of the words in this book it would be 10,000 km (6210 miles) long.

CHROMOSOMES

Growing places

Your relatives might think you've grown quite a bit in the last year but that's nothing to the amount of growing you did before you were born. You probably can't remember that far back – so here's what happened.

Most animals mate to make new offspring. (The only creatures that don't are tiny jelly-like things that you can only see through a microscope. They split in two – which

151

sounds really painful.) But we humans also mate to make children. Well, just imagine your poor parents having to split in two to make your little brother!

The aim of mating is to allow the male and female parents to mix their genes up. That's why children end up looking a bit like both their parents.

THAT'S OUR BOY!

The genes are carried in special cells called sperm and eggs. The male makes sperm cells in his testes and the female releases an egg cell from her ovaries. (In humans the egg cell is far smaller than a hen's egg – in fact you need a microscope to see it at all!) The male releases 400,000,000 tiny tadpole-like sperm at a time but only one of these manages to dive into the egg to make a baby.

Baby-builders

The egg now divides into two cells, and these divide to make 4, 8, 16, 32, 64, 128, 256, 512, 1,024, 2,048, 4,096, 8,192, 16,384, 32,768, 65,536 cells and so on. (You continue this list if you really want!)

So from two original cells come all the cells in the body – your muscles, bones, teeth, brain, liver, eyeballs, sweat-glands and everything else. This process of division and sorting goes on until the tiny ball of cells turns into a baby. A tiny, incredible, brand-new human being.

Incredible infancy

Now you might think that babies are pretty useless and definitely disgusting. After all, they do nothing much except sleep, dribble, throw up and other unmentionable things. But babies are incredible (just ask their mums and dads!) and babyhood is an incredible time for the body. Which of the following are too amazing to be true?

1 In the 238 days before birth a baby's weight increases 5 million times. (Lucky you don't put on weight so quickly nowadays!) TRUE / FALSE

UMBILICAL CORD

2 During this time a baby floats around happily in a salty pool inside it's mum's womb. It turns somersaults and even scratches itself with its fingernails. TRUE / FALSE

BABY AFTER 36 WEEKS

CAN'T WAIT TO STRETCH MY LEGS!

3 The baby is fed from the mother through a tube called the umbilical cord that passes through its belly button. TRUE / FALSE

4 Babies go through a stage before they are born when they are covered in tiny hairs. TRUE / FALSE

5 Babies have a natural sense of rhythm. They kick their little hands and feet in time to music even before they are born. TRUE / FALSE

6 When they are born babies can't see in colour, only in

black and white. TRUE / FALSE

7 Babies can taste food better than grown-ups because they have about 9,000 more taste-buds. TRUE / FALSE

8 Babies can remember faces. TRUE / FALSE

9 A baby can tell when someone is talking in a foreign language. TRUE / FALSE

10 Babies sleep more but dream less than adults. TRUE / FALSE

Answers: 1-4 TRUE **5-6** FALSE But unborn babies do kick in response to loud noises! **7-9** TRUE **10** FALSE Babies dream more.

In the first year after they are born, babies get 6.3 kg (1 stone) heavier. Within two years they can walk and talk. At five they're old enough to go to school. And after that it's downhill all the way.

MY BABY!

Appalling old age

Age does funny things to people. The older a grown-up gets the less willing they are to admit how old they are. You might think that your teacher is about 98. But if you dare to ask him he might well say, "I'm in the prime of life." (Teachers are ALIVE?!) Well anyway, here are a few sure signs of ageing to look out for in your teachers.

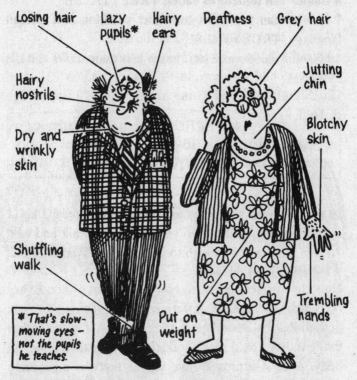

Losing hair

Lazy pupils*

Hairy ears

Deafness

Grey hair

Hairy nostrils

Dry and wrinkly skin

Jutting chin

Blotchy skin

Shuffling walk

* That's slow-moving eyes – not the pupils he teaches.

Put on weight

Trembling hands

AMAZING old age

BUT don't assume that your poor old teacher is a clapped-out old has-been. Remember . . . older people (and that includes your more mature teachers) have a vast store of wisdom and learning. Many famous people have made their greatest contribution to world history in their later years.

• Genghis Khan (1162-1227) the Mongolian soldier was

conquering most of the known world when he was in his sixties.

• William Gladstone (1809-1898) was Prime Minister of Britain when he was in his eighties.

• In a single year, English novelist Barbara Cartland wrote 26 books. She was 82 at the time.

• Shirali Mislimov of Georgia was born in 1806 and his youngest child was born in 1937 when he was 131. And Old Shirali was still going strong in 1973 at the age of 168!

MY BIRTHDAY CAKES ARE STARTING TO LOOK A BIT SILLY!

The horrible truth

Nobody's perfect. And no body is perfect either. Every body ages, aches and suffers from disgusting diseases. Sometimes its bones get broken, too. A few scientists thought they could make something better than a human body. A new improved home-made body or a machine that could replace the body.

156

But was it worth the effort? For all its faults, the body is the most fantastic, the most incredible machine in the entire universe. And it's all yours! Your body can do things that no machine could ever do. It can grow, and when it works harder its muscles grow too. It can walk thousands of kilometres and not wear out. The soles of its feet even renew themselves and thicken to make walking easier.

Your body can do 101 different things, and the most amazing thing of all is that you can do them ALL AT ONCE!

- You can ride a bicycle and digest your dinner.

- Kick a football and imagine you're playing in the Cup Final.

- You can listen to music and do your homework and still guzzle a packet of crisps!

The body suffers from disgusting diseases, it's true. But then it gets better. It actually heals and repairs itself. All you have to do is to give it proper food and exercise. Treat your body well and it'll last a lifetime.

Of course, if you went into Baron Frankenstein's lab and saw all the body bits, the bones and bottles of blood you might say, "Yuck! How horrible!"

But you've also got to admit that the body is more than just horrible. It's horribly amazing too! And that's horrible science for you!

HORRIBLE SCIENCE

Science with the squishy bits left in!

Ugly Bugs
Blood, Bones and Body Bits
Nasty Nature
Chemical Chaos
Fatal Forces
Sounds Dreadful
Evolve or Die
Vicious Veg
Disgusting Digestion
Bulging Brains
Frightening Light
Shocking Electricity
Deadly Diseases
Microscopic Monsters
Killer Energy
The Body Owner's Handbook
The Terrible Truth About Time
Space, Stars and Slimy Aliens
Painful Poison
The Fearsome Fight For Flight
Angry Animals

Specials
Suffering Scientists
Explosive Experiments
The Awfully Big Quiz Book
Really Rotten Experiments

Two horrible books in one
Ugly Bugs and Nasty Nature
Blood, Bones and Body Bits and Chemical Chaos
Frightening Light and Sounds Dreadful
Bulging Brains and Disgusting Digestion
Microscopic Monsters and Deadly Diseases